W9-BUZ-438

O😐PS!

13 MANAGEMENT PRACTICES THAT WASTE TIME AND MONEY *(and what to do instead)*

O⬤PS!

13 MANAGEMENT PRACTICES THAT WASTE TIME AND MONEY *(and what to do instead)*

aubrey c. daniels

BEST SELLING AUTHOR OF *BRINGING OUT THE BEST IN PEOPLE*

Performance Management Publications (PMP)

PMP

Performance Management Publications (PMP)
3344 Peachtree Road NE, Suite 1050
Atlanta, GA 30326
678.904.6140
www.PManagementPubs.com

ISBN-13: 978-0-937100-17-2

ISBN-10: 0-937100-17-X

2 3 4 5 6 7

Cover and text design: Lisa Smith
Editor: Gail Snyder
Administrative Editor: Brenda Jernigan
Production Coordinator: Laura-Lee Glass
Set in Cheltenham

PMP books are available at special discounts for bulk purchases by
corporations, institutions, and other organizations. For more information,
please call 678.904.6140, ext. 131 or e-mail lglass@aubreydaniels.com

DEDICATION

In the hope that the workplace they enter
will have embraced the science of behavior,
I dedicate this book to my grandchildren:

Elijah Houston Senter

Liam Daniels Glass

Aubrey Olivia Senter

ACKNOWLEDGMENTS

Althea Gibson said, "No matter what accomplishments you make, somebody helped you." As always it takes many people to write books and I have been blessed by having the assistance of many talented people help me with this one.

I am particularly indebted to Tom Critchfield who made many edits of both content and organization of the text and is an outstanding editor as well as scholar in the science of behavior, behavior analysis. Gail Snyder and Brenda Jernigan have assisted me with my previous books and did their usual excellent job of editing my grammar and thereby making the book substantially more readable than it would have been otherwise. Darnell Lattal not only provided me with encouragement in the beginning and positive reinforcement throughout the entire process but also made many valuable suggestions about the content. Jeff Sims and Rich Gold provided many helpful edits from the perspective of executives who work every day to implement the ideas included in this book in their organizations. They are not only outstanding practitioners, but are also outstanding students of the science. Laura Lee Glass managed the entire production process and was most accommodating in helping me meet a tight production schedule. Lisa Smith designed the cover and completed the layout of the work in record time.

Others who read the manuscript and offered many helpful suggestions are: Cloyd Hyten, Jon Bailey, Sherman Roberts, Joe Laipple, Bart Sevin, Ken Wagner, Joe Wiley, Tom Spencer, Matt Porritt, Jerry Pounds, Jack Connolly, and Jeanine Plowman.

Finally, I can do little without the valuable assistance of Sandy Stewart. She has been my second left hand (I'm left-handed) for over 38 years. She knows me so well that she not only finishes my sentences but starts many of them as well. She makes everything I do easier and I am fortunate to have her as a friend and business associate for all these years.

CONTENTS

PREFACE

Beware of false knowledge;
it is more dangerous than ignorance.

–George Bernard Shaw

In a cost-cutting move in March 2007, electronics retailer Circuit City laid off all sales associates who were paid 51 cents or more per hour above an established pay range, essentially firing 3400 of its top performers. It is probably not coincidence that the stock dropped 70 percent in the next eight months. Interestingly, the stock price jumped 2 percent to $19.23 at the announcement of Circuit City's firing spree, but as of September 26, 2008 it was trading at $1.37. On that day the president resigned amidst the plummeting stock price and shareholder calls for his ouster. As Jay Leno might say, "What were they thinking?" It would be interesting to know how the company executives made the decision to terminate their highest paid associates. Did it never occur to them that the highest paid sales associates just might be their best sales associates? Did they believe that this action would have the effect of energizing the remaining associates? What knowledge of human behavior did they draw upon to make this decision?

This example is only one of the *101 Dumbest Moments in Business* for 2007 as reported in *Fortune* magazine. Notice that the magazine reported only 101 of the dumbest moments, but many more similar examples were probably available. In fact, during my last 40 years working with organizations around the world, I have witnessed many "What were they thinking?" moments. The problem is not that managers make mistakes in dealing with people. The problem is that because they do not have scientific knowledge of behavior, they do not understand how their decisions will influence the behavior of the people who must implement those decisions. Therefore, they continue to make the same mistakes. In many cases these performance-killing mistakes have been institutionalized into policies and procedures, into training for new managers and even incorporated into pay, appraisal and motivational systems as well.

Even today, when executives should know better, the common approach to financial management is to cut employees across the board. Implicit in such decisions is the belief that employees cannot help management achieve the goals necessary to make the business profitable. Amazingly, employees are still viewed as a cost rather than a solution. Yet every CEO in this country has stood before employees and declared, "People are our most important asset." Then they dispose of the company's most important asset the minute the organization is in trouble. Until executives understand behavior from a scientific perspective, ineffective management practices and systems, and faulty decision making will continue to have serious negative impact on revenue and earnings.

This book is guided by a simple reality: people's actions (behaviors) are the central determinant of business success. There is good news and bad news to report about this reality. The good news is that human behavior has been studied for over 100 years. We know a great deal about how it works and what is required to make it work better. The bad news is that the scientific study of behavior rarely is addressed in business school curricula; similarly, knowledge of behavior rarely is a requirement for taking on business leadership positions.

Albert Einstein reportedly commented that the world's problems cannot be solved by the same kind of thinking that created them. The science of behavior does not offer all of the answers that managers might want but most certainly it can help us to rise above the kind of thinking that led to the Circuit City debacle.

This book, then, is about better management. As *Fortune's* list of dumbest moments illustrates, opportunities for improvement abound, but I have chosen to address 13 practices that are especially cherished by managers. The practices are in no particular order. I chose to list them in an order that will hopefully be interesting to you. After you read the first two chapters, you need not read them consecutively, but read them in the order that you find most interesting or relevant to your work.

In the following pages, I will point out problems associated with each of the 13 practices, and for each I will propose practical and effective fixes. Each critique of the management practices in this book is verified by extensive behavioral research. I cannot, however, cover the complete science of behavior in this book. As a matter of fact, I will attempt to use very few technical terms, though I will present some basic facts about behavior and explain behavioral solutions that are easy to apply. Keep an open mind about what constitutes a good management practice—and remember that a good management practice incorrectly implemented can be just as harmful as a bad management practice implemented correctly.

As you read this book, I hope that soon, you will begin to understand how to assess and avoid such mistakes yourself and you will see just how much you can improve your business by understanding and using the knowledge of human behavior to improve workplace results.

INTRODUCTION

A dull tool works but a sharp one works better.
–Anon

This book brings into question management practices that have been used for at least a century and in many cases practiced almost universally. I learned long ago that in management, just because something doesn't work, doesn't mean managers won't continue to use it. And just because something does work, doesn't mean people will use it. For example, in the book *Moneyball* (2003), author Michael Lewis convincingly shows that major league baseball has been managing and rewarding the wrong behaviors for over 100 years. Based on the work of Bill James, baseball historian and statistician, Lewis explains that many of the measures on which players are selected for the major leagues, and the measures on which player effectiveness and compensation are based, are wrong. James' work, and the work of Earnshaw Cook before him, is based on a statistical analysis of many years of statistical data on every aspect of the game. Even so, the majority of baseball people initially rejected these findings outright, not on the merit of the research but because the studies challenge a traditional way of managing.[i]

Frank Deford, a prominent sportswriter, explained why most teams have been reluctant to accept these findings when he reviewed *Earnshaw Cook's Percentage Baseball (1966)*. He says, "Right now . . . Earnshaw Cook knows more about baseball than anyone else in the world . . . baseball officials hesitate to consider his findings, and for a very good reason: if he is right, they have been playing the game all wrong for years."

Is it also possible that we have been managing all wrong for years?

How can enterprises survive for years, even decades, while managing in a way that is far from optimal? Actually, in baseball it is easy. Since all teams used the same management system, none had an advantage, or disadvantage. The same thing holds true for a large number of management practices designed to impact the behavior of people in the workplace. If all businesses are using the same basic pay system, appraisal system, and recognition system, how would you know whether those practices are the best or the worst? While it is true that there are a number of variations between systems, it is also possible that the differences are inconsequential. If the annual performance appraisal system is basically flawed, using the same system on a quarterly basis

---

[i] Bill James was hired by the Boston Red Sox in 2003 and is considered to have been instrumental in helping the Sox break an 86-year drought in winning the World Series, winning in 2004 and 2007.

doesn't make it better; it makes it worse! If pay and appraisal systems aren't tied to bottom-line performance, the differences between them don't matter that much.

One might argue that the reason pay, appraisal, and recognition systems are so similar is because they are the most effective. I would argue that while most widely used practices and systems have some obvious advantages, those advantages do not necessarily create the highest value for the organization and have rarely been tested scientifically. These practices are designed based on a wide range of philosophies of what it takes to motivate, control, and manage large numbers of people. The strategies used to implement them are complex and often require many people to manage them. They are based on theories of performance that have little to do with the science of learning. As such, they are at the heart of many large missteps initiated by senior leadership at great cost, endorsed for the best of reasons, but failing to lead to the desired impact.

In my seminars people have asked me, "Now when you made this up . . ." I stop them and say, "Wait a minute; I didn't make this up anymore than Sir Isaac Newton made up gravity." Behavior analysis has a history that goes back to the late 1800s. Many people have spent, and continue to spend, their entire careers solely studying human behavior. I have spent 48 years of my life studying behavior and the last 40 helping others apply the research findings to employee behavior in the workplace.

Since 1978 Aubrey Daniels International (ADI) has been helping organizations use the science of human behavior to gain competitive advantage by creating a workplace that captures the discretionary effort of all employees. As a testament to the power of managing behavior effectively, we have been successful in spite of the fact that many of the gains have occurred in organizations where existing systems and management practices are behaviorally flawed.

For example, I have often chided managers in the nuclear power industry about the fact that, in an industry based on the science of physics, many managers continue to make decisions about human behavior based on a majority vote. No one in management asks for scientific data or research on behavioral changes they intend to make as they certainly would when making some technical changes in how they produce electricity from a nuclear reactor. Instead, when it comes to human performance, they ask for opinions. They do not look systematically at the behavior in front of them as a reflection of the performance environment that they have created, but rather as a reflection of the employee's internal motivation to do a good or poor job.

TWO REASONS WHY BEHAVIOR SCIENCE IS IGNORED

WHO KNEW?

A major reason that most managers tend not to ask for behavioral data is that they have not had exposure to behavior analysis, the science of behavior. For reasons that are too complex to explain here, most of what business schools teach about psychology has little to do with the practical challenges that managers face, and most of what they teach about behavioral psychology is wrong.[ii]

Since only a very few universities teach business students behavior analysis, it is understandable that most of the business systems and practices that managers design to motivate employees are based on other ideas—often ideas derived

---

[ii] Examples include factual errors, such as that research shows positive reinforcement is harmful to motivation, and preposterous urban legends, such as that a major figure in behavioral psychology, B. F. Skinner, conducted experiments on his daughter and thereby drove her mad!

from daily operating experience. Yet, experience is not always a good teacher as Benjamin Franklin noted years ago when he said, "Experience is a dear school and fools will learn in no other." Therefore, analyzing the impact of behavior on processes and systems and vice versa is not a skill-set that most managers possess.

It almost never fails that an executive in one of my seminars will ask me, "Why aren't the business schools teaching this?" The answer is rather long, but the short answer is that if what you are doing is working, there is little motivation to change. The problem with this line of reasoning concerns the operational definition of "working." For businesses, it might mean that business schools teach practices that are commonly used. For business school professors, it may mean that it is easy to continue to teach the same material if the students aren't complaining (and few complain to the professor). Whatever the explanation, the result is unfortunate, since the incredible business impact that can be achieved by understanding human behavior and applying that knowledge effectively is rarely known or experienced by the college business major.

As is turns out, the behavioral (as opposed to cognitive) approach is significantly more efficient and effective in producing results in the workplace than the many alternatives. For the evidence, see *Performance Management Magazine,* the *Journal of Organizational Behavior Management,* as well as the books listed in the Suggested Readings section at the end of this book. All of these publications have documented many highly successful applications for well over 30 years.

MONEY SYSTEMS VS. PEOPLE SYSTEMS

Another reason many organizational systems are behaviorally flawed is that they were originally designed by those who were first and foremost concerned with the economic health of the organization, primarily financial personnel. How employees were paid, appraised, rewarded, and recognized had financial implications. When designed without an understanding of behavior, these systems can be expensive and minimally effective in terms of affecting employee performance. When the wrong behaviors are inadvertently rewarded by a financially sound compensation plan, that plan will never be effective or efficient.

Just because employees are paid a lot of money doesn't mean that they produce the best value for the company. For example, Bucklin and Dickinson (2001) have shown that there is not a positive correlation between the size of a bonus and productivity. The bonuses and golden parachutes taken by the top executives of failed companies are prime examples of that fact! Many organizations have learned that just because you have a good financial and benefit package for employees, union or non-union, doesn't guarantee that you will create valuable performance by all, or even most, employees. For example, a plant out West was losing some of its top performers and management decided that they needed to do something to stop the outflow. They spent one million dollars on a bonus for the top 10 percent of their managers only to find out later that 95 percent of them were unhappy. This obviously meant that at least half of those who got the bonuses were unhappy! This is not a good way to spend a million bucks.

Let me quickly add here that it is not my intention that employees should earn less but just the opposite. When money is used wisely, employees can take home more pay while the company enjoys higher profits. Bill Abernathy (2000), a behavioral workplace specialist, showed that in 12 companies using his behaviorally sound pay-for-performance system, the performance increase in the first year averaged 33.1 percent. In this system, high-performing employees earned 20-30 percent above their industry average. Also, a

Towers-Perrin Global Workforce Study (2007-2008) showed that companies with the most engaged employees had a 12 month earnings per share growth that was 39 percent greater than those with the least engaged employees.[iii] If management practices, systems, and processes are not designed on the basis of known facts about behavior, no organization can expect to create a workplace where all employees consistently give their best. This is the only way the organization can produce the best products or services at the lowest price while achieving the best return to the stakeholders. There is no other subject as important to leadership as that of learning about behavior.

o   o   o   o   o   o

[iii] *Engagement* is a non-specific, non-scientific term used to describe the amount of positive reinforcement available in a workplace for value-added behavior.

WHAT ALL MANAGERS NEED TO KNOW ABOUT BEHAVIOR

"Science is like a river, flowing inexorably downstream,
freshened and swollen by rivulets of data.
Our attempts to dam or divert it are too puny to prevail for long
against the gathering weight;
sooner or later all obstacles are swept away,
and the river resumes its natural course.
We can force Galileo to recant, but we cannot force the earth
to stand still; eventually the astronomer is vindicated."

–David Palmer

BUSINESS IS BEHAVIOR

From a business or organizational perspective, the most important thing we know about behavior is that it is the only way that any organization's outcomes are accomplished. Employees design, develop, and deliver services and products; managers give employees instructions and feedback; accountants tabulate earnings and expenses; and so forth. At the heart of everything a business does are things that people do and say: behavior. Upon reflection, this should be obvious. However, if everything about behavior were obvious, we would not need a science of human behavior. Science begins with the obvious, but because human behavior is so varied, and often comes at you so fast, it is often difficult to discern the cause-and-effect relationships that make behavior occur as it does. Only through carefully controlled studies replicated many times under varying conditions have lawful relationships been discovered.

From 100 years of scientific discovery, scientists have accumulated knowledge about behavior that fills countless volumes. There is still much to learn, but fortunately, one does not need to know everything about a subject before what is known can be put to practical use. For example, André-Marie Ampère discovered the relationship between electricity and magnetism in 1820 and just one year later, Michael Faraday invented the electric motor. Even though we have learned much about electricity since, people continue to do research to learn more. The same is true of behavior. The principles of behavior are just as much a part of human nature as gravity and electricity. While there is much yet to learn about behavior, what we have learned can be used to make significant improvements, not only in the workplace, but in all areas of life.

BEHAVIOR AS A STRATEGIC SUCCESS FACTOR

Business leaders are taught many things that are critical to the success of an organization, but the idea that the most important thing a corporate executive should know is how to change behavior at the individual, group, and national levels is rarely taught. Certainly executives are not expected to change behavior at those levels; but without an understanding of how behavior change takes place, policies, procedures, and systems are often approved and implemented in ways that cause employees to underperform.

In a great many organizations, human resources is given the impossible task of introducing and even implementing initiatives, policies, and systems that will properly capture employee motivation; but, in every case I know, the HR professionals constantly refer to the need for understanding and support from the highest level of the organization.

Whether employees perform at their best or something less is due to the interface of behavior with the systems, policies, management processes, and practices approved at the top of the corporation. If this interface is punishing rather than reinforcing the discretionary behavior, on which high performing organizations depend, will not occur. In every organization employees are frustrated daily by policies and practices that create obstacles rather than facilitate the behavior required to do an outstanding job. When managers and executives do not understand behavior as a scientific subject, one poorly implemented initiative may be substituted for another. Frequently good strategic plans fail because of poor execution. If executives are not able to separate the plan from the execution (behavior), they often make the mistake of changing the strategic plan when the execution is at fault. As Larry Bossidy stated in his book, *Execution: The Discipline of Getting Things Done* (2002), "To put it simply and starkly: If you don't get the people process right, you will never fulfill the potential of your business." The people process is nothing more than behaviors organized toward a specific organizational result. Getting the right behaviors to occur at the right time in the right way and at the right frequency is what separates the successful strategies from the unsuccessful ones.

Some things we know about human behavior

RULE-GOVERNED VS. CONTINGENCY-SHAPED BEHAVIOR

Behavior can be contingency-shaped or rule-governed. Contingency shaped means that the person learns from direct experience with the consequences of his or her actions. You touch a hot stove and learn from the immediate sensation of pain that this is not a good thing to do. Once learned, most contingency-shaped behavior continues to exist because it is intermittently reinforced. For example, consequences mattered when you first learned to speak clearly (e.g., people gave you what you wanted). **Speaking clearly** continues to matter in part because, when you do, people sometimes give you what you want. When you don't speak clearly, people may give you the wrong thing or nothing at all because they didn't know what you said. Speaking clearly is an example of contingency-shaped responding.

Rule-governed behavior means that the person learns indirectly, without direct contact with consequences. Under rule-governed behavior, the person does not need to experience the consequence directly but learns by reading or observing others. The humorist, Will Rogers, identified two kinds of rule-governed behavior when he observed that, "There are three kinds of men: the ones who learn by reading, a few who learn by observation and the rest of them have to pee on the electric fence and find out for themselves." Here, the encounter with the electric fence is an example of contingency-shaping. Reading and observation in this case allow learning without more painful ways of testing for yourself what others have learned the hard way. Finding a light switch in a dark room is contingency shaped. You feel about the wall until the switch is found and flipped. Putting a toy or new piece of equipment together without reading the instructions is contingency-shaped and is almost always an inefficient way to accomplish the task.

A rule about vending machines can be learned by someone telling you as you approach the machine that it is broken. You have probably learned from your experience that when someone tells you a machine is broken you can save time and effort (and possibly a little bit of money) by listening to what they say. Thus, you would not have to put coins in this particular machine to learn whether it works.

Importantly, rules can be formal or informal. Policy manuals contain formal rules like, "Disengage the electrical supply before servicing the equipment," while an informal rule may be, "Don't break in line." Rules also may be public or private. Management memoranda often declare public rules such as "Work starts promptly at eight o'clock," and a private rule may be something that you say to yourself, such as "I always turn out the lights when leaving an empty room."

When we are young, following rules itself is a form of contingency-shaped behavior. Sometimes we follow the rules that our parents and others give us, and often the outcome is good. Sometimes we don't follow those rules, and often the outcome is bad. Eventually, because of the consequences we experience, we become capable of following many kinds of rules.

Once we begin following a particular rule, whether we *continue* to follow it depends on the consequences that flow from rule-following. Speed limit signs imply the rule that driving at speeds above the limit will result in a speeding ticket. However, since very few drivers who speed get tickets (the implied consequence), the signs are largely ignored. By contrast, children who have been taught the rules of good manners early in life will likely maintain these behaviors throughout life because of frequent naturally-occurring consequences; that is, they will experience many social advantages that follow from using good manners. Unfortunately, organizations have many rules that are not followed because employees do not experience the intended consequence frequently enough to make the rule effective.

Certainly rules are an efficient way to run an organization; however, very often little attention is paid to making sure that the stated or implied consequences follow the rules consistently enough to maintain their integrity. If an employee frequently sees other employees leaving early, he may begin to leave early even though the rule is to leave at 5 p.m. There may be a rule to wear personal protective equipment in hazardous areas, but if the rule is not consistently enforced many people will work without it.

Contingency-shaped behavior is often thought of as *learning the hard way.* You have heard it often: "You can't tell him anything, he will just have to learn it for himself." Indeed, especially as children there are many things that we learn only through direct experience. Learning to walk and talk is almost completely contingency-shaped. Infants don't know the rules and have to fall many times to master the skill of walking. As adults, however, most of what we learn is the result of a combination of rules and reinforcement contingencies. Research on behavioral fluency shows that when people have a history of frequent positive reinforcement for knowing and following rules, they are not only able to make quick and effective decisions involving day-to-day matters, but are also able to be innovative and creative when such decisions are required. Since rule governed behavior is considerably more efficient than contingency shaped behavior—it sets behavior change into motion more quickly—organizations that know how to establish effective rules are in a more competitive position than those that don't.

SOME THINGS WE KNOW ABOUT CONSEQUENCES

The preceding shows that consequences matter to rule-following just as they do to contingency-shaped behavior. In short, whether their behavior is rule-governed or contingency-shaped, people learn from consequences. The closest thing we have to a behavioral law, as gravity is a law of physics, is: *Behavior is a function of its consequences.* Science teaches us that there are four types of behavioral consequences. Here are some things we know, with a high degree of certainty, about how they affect behavior.

- Two types of consequences, positive and negative reinforcement, increase existing behaviors and can be used to teach new ones.

- Positive reinforcement produces higher rates of behavior than negative reinforcement.

- A small, immediate consequence has more impact on behavior than a large, future, and uncertain one.

- Behavior that occurs without reinforcement is weakened and will eventually stop.

- Two types of consequences, punishment and penalty, stop existing behaviors. They don't increase behavior, and they teach no new ones.

- Behavior that is stopped by punishment and penalty will reoccur when the threat of punishment or penalty is removed or is remote.

By systematically harnessing these facts, behavior scientists have promoted many practical and effective applications. Unfortunately, as the remaining chapters of this book explain, many management practices and systems are designed and implemented in ways that run counter to these facts regarding behavior and as such waste time and money.

SOME THINGS WE KNOW ABOUT POSITIVE REINFORCEMENT

Positive reinforcement is any consequence that follows a behavior and increases its frequency. This is a very important fact to know. What this means is that if you tell someone she is doing a good job and the behavior you intended to increase did not increase, then what you did was not a positive reinforcer for that behavior even though that was what you intended. We cannot say that money, telling someone that he is doing a good job, or giving an attaboy is a reinforcer. They are only reinforcers if they increase behavior. However, if what you said or did was a reinforcer, it will have increased some behavior even though it may not have been the one you wanted.

I have said many times that positive reinforcement is the most powerful interpersonal concept known and it is also the most misunderstood and misused. For example, "Always be positive" is the worst advice you could ever give or get because if you are positive at the wrong time you are very likely to get more of the wrong behavior. It is my opinion that most of the world's problems are caused by positive reinforcement. Terrorism is fueled by positive reinforcement. (News reports tying a bombing to a particular group help recruiting and increase funding). The wasting of natural resources is caused by positive reinforcement. (Driving fast wastes gasoline but gets you where you want to go sooner.) Ethnic conflicts and revolutions are fought over attempts to gain access to positive reinforcers. (Tribal conflicts in Iraq and elsewhere are over land, oil reserves, and political power.) Positive reinforcement is like nuclear power. It can be used to heal you or kill you. Misunderstood and misused, positive reinforcement can produce economic, political, and social disasters. Properly used, it can create a future of unlimited achievement.

Although positive reinforcement is not the only consequence used in the workplace, it is the most important because it is the only one that creates the highest value for an organization. It changes the way managers look at their jobs as well. If managers learn that positive reinforcement solves problems quicker, better, and with less stress, they no longer need to resort to command and control and a *do it or else* style of management. Management is about arranging conditions for the optimal success of everyone (and, ultimately, the organization). Leadership is measured against the success of every single follower in an organization. Both management and leadership require a very skilled application of positive reinforcement.

MAKING BEHAVIOR WORK

Positive reinforcement always works. I have discovered over the years that when someone claims that "reinforcement didn't work" they have made one or more errors in either the selection or delivery of the reinforcer. These errors can be avoided by doing the following.

1. **Make it personal**. People are unique in the things they find reinforcing. Although many people may find the same things to be reinforcing, not everyone will. For example, a large percentage of people at work find money to be highly reinforcing but, believe it or not, some people have all they need or want (and they are not all rich). Therefore, the offer of money as a positive reinforcer for some behavior will not be motivating to such people. Employees often turn down overtime pay because they value their free time more than they value more money.

2. **Make it contingent.** To be most effective, positive reinforcers must be earned. There must be a direct link between behavior and the delivery of the reinforcer. The best test of this is to ask the question, "What did the person have to do to earn the reinforcer?" The critical word is *earn*. As you will see, many of the benefits, rewards and even compensation that people receive at work are often not for an accomplishment but for being in the right place at the right time. Benefits are typically rewards for being on the payroll. Raises may be given to everyone on an annual basis. Cost of living adjustments are given across the board. And so it goes.

3. **Make it immediate.** While it is difficult for most people to understand, positive reinforcement increases the behavior that is occurring when one gets it. Reinforcement that is delayed is likely to increase the behavior occurring when the positive reinforcer is delivered rather than the behavior that it was intended to reinforce. We learn to be superstitious because a behavior, such as re-pushing the button for the elevator, coincides with the arrival of the elevator when there is, in fact, no causal relation between the re-pushing and the speed of arrival. A child, who has earned a reward but receives it only after he starts crying for it, is reinforced for crying, not for what he did to earn it.

4. **Make it frequent.** One positive reinforcer will not make a habit. Many reinforcers are needed to establish a habit. Video games deliver over 100 reinforcers per minute to the players. Compare that to annual, quarterly, and monthly attempts at reward and recognition that most corporations use to try to create high levels of motivation.

NEGATIVE REINFORCEMENT IS A DIFFICULT CONCEPT TO MASTER

One misunderstanding about negative reinforcement is that it is often confused with punishment. Some business writers have presented negative reinforcement and punishment as the same thing with different names. However, they are very different in their effects on behavior. The basic difference is that punishment decreases behavior whereas negative reinforcement increases it.

Another misunderstanding is that because both positive and negative reinforcement increase behavior, it is often difficult for those unfamiliar with the science to determine which consequence produced the increase. From a leadership or organizational perspective, understanding the difference is critical to getting the best out of people. Negative reinforcement trades on punishment; that is, people will do enough to escape or avoid punishment, but once the punishment is avoided or escaped, there is no motivation to do more. Think about walking through a railroad tunnel when you see a train entering the other end of the tunnel. Undoubtedly you turn and run as fast as you can until you get out of the tunnel. At that point you jump off the track and stop running because there is no benefit in continuing to run. Apply this effect to business issues. Anytime people do something because they *have to* rather than because they *want to,* their behavior is under negative reinforcement control. If your parents ever told you that you studied "just enough to get by" they were describing a situation where neither your parents nor the teacher had made studying positively reinforcing. It is a fact that most organizations are managed by negative reinforcement, not by design or intent but because they don't understand the difference between the two kinds of reinforcement.

Negative reinforcement is the default form of reinforcement. That is to say that if people are performing without positive reinforcement, the behavior is being managed by negative reinforcement since that is the only other way to generate behavior. Where managers expect employees to perform to certain standards because that is what they are paid to do is a classic example of negative reinforcement. The *most* you will get in such situations is the standard performance. Initiative, ownership, buy-in, and volunteerism are almost never produced by negative reinforcement. Because these behavioral characteristics are so important to the success of the modern organization, few organizations can afford the drag on performance produced by negative reinforcement.

THE ADVANTAGE OF AN IN-DEPTH UNDERSTANDING OF BEHAVIOR

Behavior **is** time and money. Failure to understand human behavior from a scientific perspective costs organizations serious money and causes significant morale problems. All of the 13 practices, systems, and procedures included in this book were originally designed to change work behavior in a positive way—to get employees to be more productive, coop-erative, enthusiastic, creative, and innovative. However, most of the 13 have their genesis in what is popularly called "com-mon sense" or based on an individual leader or manager's experiences. Few if any were designed on the basis of valid and proven research in human behavior.

For example, when people say that they "already know positive reinforcement," maybe to an extent they do. However, most of them know it only to the extent that they know gravity. What most people know about gravity is that objects released above the ground will fall toward the earth, but most people don't know gravity as it affects objects in motion. When will a speeding car start to drop when running off a cliff? Will it continue on the same trajectory for a dis-tance determined by the speed or will it start to drop imme-diately independent of the speed? When asked where a ball would land if dropped by a walking person, only 45 percent of college students knew the ball would travel forward as it fell (McClosky, 1983). Dave Pelz, renowned professional golf instructor, has shown that most golfers misjudge the line of a breaking putt, almost always underestimating how much the putt will break.

As it relates to human behavior, people's understanding is about the same. They know that positive reinforcement works at some level: you get more flies with honey than vinegar. However, they don't know that yelling and screaming at a person could be a positive reinforcer or that telling someone that he is doing a good job could be a punisher. It is my opinion that in today's competitive, global marketplace those who know behavior in depth will eventually be the winners.

Francis Bacon asserted "We cannot command nature except by obeying her." Like gravity, like electricity, behavior will unfold as nature has proscribed, regardless of what we intend or whether we are aware of the underlying processes. In organizations, what is reinforced is what gets done. Therefore, if we build organizations consistent with what we know—that is, if we understand and *correctly* apply some of the basic facts mentioned above—the principles of behavior will contribute to a dramatically improved workplace. If we don't apply what is known, then nature will play out anyway, and the results will always be less than optimal.

o   o   o   o   o   o

THE 13
MANAGEMENT PRACTICES
THAT WASTE TIME AND MONEY

#1
EMPLOYEE OF THE MONTH (EOM)
(and most other forms of recognition and reward)

There are cheaper ways to upset people.

–John Cochran

Selecting an employee for special recognition every month, quarter, or year is the most common form of workplace recognition. As far as I can determine, the purpose of the practice, which I will refer to as Employee of the Month (EOM) is to motivate employees to do their best. I can state categorically that it doesn't. Managers and supervisors apparently assume that those who don't get the recognition (which is everybody but one person) will be motivated to try to earn the recognition the next month. That assumption also is dead wrong. As a matter of fact, EOM violates every known principle of effective positive reinforcement.

A Web article (The Onion, 2000) satirizing Employee of the Month programs—"Employee of the Month Sad It's Already the 19th"—nonetheless illustrates the real problems with the practice. A woman, who was the current EOM in a 97-employee retail store in Tennessee, complained that the month of her award was almost half over. She said, "Before you know it I will be just another employee again." In spite of that she also complained about the pressure she felt being "in the spotlight," because "there are those few jealous individuals who would just love to see you make a wrong step."

This is a common example and illustrates a few of the many problems with EOM:

1. **Reinforcement is competitive**. Recognition of one employee necessarily precludes recognizing others. In any given month, 96 employees are *just another employee.*

2. **Recognition is infrequent.** The woman described above had been working in the store for over three years before receiving the award. Across more than four years of its existence, the award had gone to a different employee every month. With 97 employees in the store, it will take over eight years for the award to make the rounds. Recognition every eight years is hardly motivational.

3. **In most organizations, recognition is not earned.** Perhaps all you have to do is to be employed long enough and eventually it will be your turn. Usually the employees cannot tell you what they have to do to get the award. Over a period of several months, I did an informal survey of 77 employees in businesses in which an EOM plaque or photo was displayed in the lobby or entrance of the building. Not one

person could tell me what he or she had to do to earn it, with a single exception. As I was renting a car from a national rental car company, I noticed an elaborate EOM display that covered the entire wall with photos of people who were selected as employee of the month, quarter, and year. I asked the woman who was helping me what one had to do to earn EOM. She stared, paused for a moment, and said, "I guess, be nice to your manager."

4. **Recognition is not reinforcing.** Recipients often are not excited about receiving EOM. Some are embarrassed by this form of attention. Others receive unpleasant attention from co-workers. Still others are simply apathetic about this kind of recognition. The owner of one business told me that he eliminated his EOM program and no one even noticed.

If this practice is not effective, what can explain its popularity? It's actually easy to understand how EOM became an imbedded recognition strategy. EOM is easy to administer, requiring only a few minutes each month to decide who will get the recognition; the person receiving it is usually excited about it, and the rewards are certainly inexpensive, requiring only a photo, a designated parking space, and possibly even a free meal or two. By the way, more elaborate and expensive awards don't increase the effectiveness; they only increase the cost. Although EOM usually is started with the best of intentions, the way the program is structured and administered assures that it will fail.

EOM: EXCEPTIONALLY OBSOLETE MANAGEMENT

Interestingly, if you ask employees if they like their organization's

EOM program most will probably answer yes. One of the reasons many employees don't mind the program is that it is of little importance to them. If you get it, ok; if you don't, no big deal. Most people feel that they will eventually be an EOM because no matter how the recognition begins, it eventually turns into a pass-around deal. This sometimes makes it difficult to discontinue the program until everyone has been EOM at least once.

Out of the Gene Pool © Matt Janz. Reprinted with Permission.

Some companies think that having the Top Ten Employees of the Month is better as it recognizes more people each month. That's even worse! It is one thing to know that you are not the best employee, but quite another to know that you didn't even make the top ten!

Some companies have employees select the EOM. This approach, which I believe is an attempt by management to avoid the problems normally associated with EOM programs, only creates more problems as employees lobby for the award or vote in cliques for their friends. Lobbying and clique voting turns EOM into a popularity contest which, over time, fractionates the employees. Of course this eliminates any notion that EOM has anything remotely to do with teamwork or hardworking or outstanding performers.

Think of it this way: the largest number of people who are impacted positively by EOM each month is exactly ONE— maybe. Sometimes the person who is selected doesn't like it because peers make fun of them or trivialize the award. Yet, the number of people who are impacted in a negative way— upset, annoyed, angered, or apathetic toward it—is always more than one. Any practice in an organization (especially a practice intended to motivate and/or reward) where more people are upset than pleased just doesn't seem productive. As one of my friends, John Cochran, says about such things, "There are cheaper ways to upset people."

To be clear, Employee of the Month fails all of the four criteria for effective positive reinforcement.

1. **EOM is not personal**. All employees get the same reward.

2. **EOM is not immediate.** The award comes weeks after the behavior.

3. **EOM is not contingent.** Since a different employee receives the recognition every month, getting it is more a matter of time rather than performance and, even more disturbing, non-contingent awards (non-earned) create a sense of entitlement.

4. **EOM is not frequent.** In the retail store mentioned previously, on average, an employee might be recognized two to three times in an entire career.

Employee of the Month fails on every criterion that behavior analysis tells us is necessary to cause people to want to do their best in the workplace every day.

REWARDS AREN'T POSITIVE IN A NEGATIVE WORKPLACE

If EOM is not effective, what about other recognition and reward programs? By their very structure recognition and reward programs, or *systems* if you prefer, cannot be frequent. This provides limited opportunities for increasing motivation. Almost all recognition systems limit in some way the number of employees who can receive the awards. While these two factors diminish the effectiveness of such systems, the single element that is the most detrimental is that such infrequent recognition is delivered to a limited number of people in workplaces where positive reinforcement from managers and supervisors is typically very sparse. All motivational systems that have one or a few winners have all the faults of EOM even though they may be called something else. Giving an award to the employee who has the best suggestion, retains the most customers, or has the highest production are all versions of EOM.

If EOM and related recognition efforts are not effective, then they certainly cannot rescue an organization from other ineffective management practices. Several years ago in a keynote speech to the National Association of Employee Recognition, (now Recognition Professionals International), the first thing I said to the group was, "Eliminate all employee reward and recognition programs." I heard the audience gasp because the job of the convention attendees was to find ways to effectively and efficiently plan and execute corporate recognition and reward programs. My point was grounded in the observation that management often is built around negative reinforcement, in which the primary motivation for employees to perform well is to avoid the threat of unpleasant outcomes such as criticism, berating, and in extreme cases, loss of their jobs. People do not manage in this way because they are mean but because they fail to see and recognize the many accomplishments that employees make every day on a moment-to-moment basis. Regardless of intent, the unpleasant work environment created by this management style more than negates any pleasantness that might be inherent in EOM or related recognition. As Tom Odom of Shell Oil Company said, "It's hard to celebrate when you have been beat-up on the way to the party."

If the primary method of management is not positively reinforcing, any attempt to recognize and reward employees creates more problems than solutions and is a waste of time and money. You can't ignore employees on a daily basis, take their accomplishments for granted, get upset when there are problems, and then expect that employees will be happy when you come out of your office at the end of the month, quarter, or year to show appreciation for what has been accomplished. An appreciative style of management is not something that you turn on and off.

 ## WHAT TO DO INSTEAD

In order to know what to do instead of EOM, answer the question, "What are you trying to accomplish?" If you are trying to do something that will reward or recognize hardworking employees, EOM doesn't. If you are trying to do something that will inspire others to work smarter or harder, EOM doesn't. If you are doing something to spotlight an employee so that other employees will get to know more about him/her, it probably does. However, it will take forever to get to everyone and there is an assumption in this practice that the person who gets EOM deserves some special recognition for work performance. Clearly, a different process is needed, so eliminate EOM as soon as possible.

Although I feel that the practice should be eliminated entirely, it could be made more effective if measurable criteria were set and *everyone* who met or exceeded the criteria received the recognition. This is unlikely to happen however, as it would be problematic from an administrative perspective and would begin to be unwieldy, since many parking spaces would be needed and checking on who was supposed to have those special spaces every month would be a chore. In addition, the number of photos and meals would begin to be expensive.

What I recommend, instead, is a *Get To Know Your Fellow Employee* program. Publish bios of every employee. Place the bios at some easily accessible spot on the internal computer system, on the Web, or put them in a book, a *Company Facebook* if you will. Employees will discover many things that they have in common with other employees and this will likely increase employee interactions that facilitate teamwork and cooperation. It may even lead to additional friendships in the workplace; something that the Gallop survey (1999) thinks is an important indicator of effective management. In addition, as people accomplish things at work, at home, or in the community that deserve some notice, put them in a newsletter or some other publication—a Did You Know? section, for example.

Ultimately, Employee of the Month carries too much negative baggage to warrant any management time and expense. So why do anything at all? You should do it because recognition and reward are valuable in a management culture of daily positive reinforcement. If you don't have a positive reinforcement culture then recognition and reward are unlikely to have the desired impact and are a waste of time and money. A positive reinforcement culture is one where everyone knows the rules for effective reinforcement and practices them every day. Positive reinforcement is not just something for managers to do. It is something that *everyone* needs to do. It is just as effective to provide positive reinforcement for your boss as it is for the boss to reinforce you.

In order to make recognition and reward effective you should:

1. **Create a positive reinforcement culture.** Focus on providing ongoing positive reinforcement for everyone who goes above and beyond their daily activities to add value to the organization.

2. **Teach all employees about positive reinforcement as a scientific concept.** When employees understand positive reinforcement as only a pat on the back or an attaboy, it is often received as superficial and insincere and therefore ineffective.

3. **Don't limit the number of employees who can be recognized and rewarded.**

4. **Set criteria such that *everyone* who exceeds the goal or standard performance is recognized and rewarded.**

5. **Avoid recognition and rewards where the adjectives, *first, top, best,* and *most improved* are used.** Avoid one winner type recognition activities like, best idea of the month, most money saved, and so on.

6. **Set the awards in such a way that you will be happiest when all employees earn them at the same time.** For example, the Mary Kay Cosmetics company has a fleet of over 9000 earned pink Cadillacs but would gladly award several times that many every year,

because the criteria for earning one are based on sales that benefit the company. Therefore, the more Cadillacs that are awarded the more successful the company becomes.

o   o   o   o   o   o

#2
STRETCH GOALS

Dream small dreams. If you make them too big,
you get overwhelmed and you don't do anything.
If you make small goals and accomplish them, it gives you
the confidence to go on to higher goals.

–John H. Johnson

Probably nothing that I say in seminars and in my books upsets more managers than saying that stretch goals are an ineffective management practice and, as such, waste time and money. This flies in the face of what they believe their own personal experience shows: that challenging employees to stretch themselves generates performance improvements. In fact, most managers have had the experience of having employees perform above the initial goal even if they didn't reach the stretch goal. So, what is the problem?

While a large amount of anecdotal evidence suggests that stretch goals work, anecdotal evidence also is the primary form of support for many ineffective products, therapies, and interventions, so it pays to look beyond testimonials (e.g., Stanovich, 2007). The objective research on stretch goals is far from conclusive. Thompson et al. (1993) point out that just stretching targets will not guarantee success—even though GE is known for extensive use of stretch goals, their early experience was so negative, they almost abandoned the initiative (Kerr and Landauer, 2004). Fisher et al. (2003) and Chow et al. (2001) found two things: employees repeatedly experienced failure in their attempts to achieve assigned goals and their performance decreased over time. Indeed, Eisenberger (1989) states, "Repeated failure for high effort causes people to become more brittle on subsequent difficult tasks, giving up quickly even when sustained performance might bring success."

In the technical language of behavior analysis, the detrimental effects of stretch goals are described in terms of *extinction*. Extinction is simply the loss of reinforcement for previously reinforced behavior. It kills motivation. Why is extinction relevant to stretch goals? Because stretch goals often are operationally defined as those that are attained less than 10 percent of the time. Missed goals are missed opportunities for reinforcement. By their very definition then, stretch goals are engineered to create extinction.

WHY MANAGERS DO THE ILLOGICAL

Given what we know about extinction, why would a manager set a goal that employees will fail to reach 90 percent of the time? One answer, of course, is that they mistakenly believe that doing so will motivate employees to achieve more than they would by only setting reasonable goals. It doesn't. What most managers fail to understand is that people are motivated only when they have received positive reinforcement for reaching their goals in the past.

Another reason managers set stretch goals is because they are constantly under pressure to make improvements, often substantial improvements. Therefore it seems only reasonable to these managers that stretch goals are the best way to push performers to do more than they think they can.

A third reason stretch goals are set is that they are consistent with popular corporate culture that believes great managers are hardnosed and demanding. Their teams are expected to reach for impossible goals or else. Yet while employees may reach and succeed on occasion, managers are effective, not through setting goals, but rather through daily actions that help employees to do the things that generate success for them and, thereby, the organization. As I have written many times, at the core of this effort is assuring that positive reinforcement is delivered for the many improvements people make on the way to goal attainment.

A CEILING ON PERFORMANCE IMPROVEMENT

When systematic positive reinforcement is lacking from goal-based systems, employee efforts are driven by negative reinforcement. They work to avoid the manger's disapproval. This is rarely a manager's intent, but because it does improve performance on some occasions, managers continue to use it. However, the improvement is limited to an amount needed to escape any negative consequences or negative reactions from the boss. Thus, negative reinforcement effectively places a ceiling on accomplishment. At best, the ceiling is just above the goal line, and when employees are lucky enough to reach this point, they stop improving. This occurs so commonly in safety that it is called the "safety plateau."

The preceding describes a best-case scenario. In reality, the ceiling may be *lower* than the goal implies. Here it is important to consider the difference between what stretch goals say and how they function. Stretch goals say that a particular level of performance is expected. But because stretch goals, by design, are rarely met, employees may learn that something less than the goal probably will be accepted. The employee may be motivated to improve less than managers assume.

Wherever the ceiling lies, it is lower when we rely on negative reinforcement than when we motivate through positive reinforcement. With negative reinforcement, motivation to improve ceases as soon as the goal is achieved. Because positive reinforcement increases with increasing achievement, performance improvement does not erode motivation. On the contrary, when things are set up right, the more employees improve the more reinforcement they can earn. The only ceiling is the ultimate one, the peak ability of the performers.

Many managers believe they can make stretch goals a positive process by letting the performers set the stretch. The assumption is that employees will be more committed to, and therefore more likely to reach, goals *they* have set. But if it is illogical for managers to set goals that employees cannot achieve, it is doubly so for employees to set such goals. Chow (2001) concluded that it is unlikely for individuals to willingly set goals for which there is a low likelihood of achievement. If employees are unwilling, but set such goals anyway, their future attempts to reach them will be driven by negative reinforcement.

From an employee's point of view, there is only one way in

which stretch goals make sense: performers have an excuse in the event of failure. If managers ask employees to set a goal that everyone knows they probably can't reach, the managers can hardly be upset if employees fail to achieve it.

THE POWER OF POSITIVE REINFORCEMENT

Sometimes in an attempt to recognize effort, managers will reward employees who worked hard and came real close but did not reach the goal. This well-intentioned practice only serves to further undermine the motivational properties of goals, because the message communicated, whether intended or not, is that reaching the goal is not all that important.

Don't get me wrong: it is *always* appropriate to provide positive reinforcement for an increase in goal-directed behavior, but this should be done on a day-to-day basis. Even if the goal is barely missed, it is not appropriate to give the rewards intended for actually achieving the goal. This is true regardless of whether managers or employees set the goals. If employees miss the goal, the manager did not provide the positive reinforcement necessary and/or set the goal too high. Even though the manager made the mistake, it does not help the organization or the employees to reward them for something they did not accomplish. Admit the mistake and correct it next time by setting highly attainable goals and by frequently reinforcing goal-related behaviors along the way.

Does this mean that we should not have lofty goals? That we should settle for something less than the best? Absolutely not! I want the company that bears my name (ADI) to exceed the highest standards. The issue is not whether we should have goals and high standards. The issue is how to get there efficiently and effectively and how to continue to make improvements.

Stretch goals are based on the faulty assumption that you have to pull performance out of people and, without repeated challenges, people will settle for something less than they are capable of doing. The remarkable thing about intelligently applied positive reinforcement is that it generates discretionary effort™. People do much more than required to simply to keep their jobs. The result can be astounding. Imagine setting a goal only to see your people blowing it away by reaching the goal in a fraction of the time set for the accomplishment or by surpassing it by two or three times the goal amount. Unfortunately, most managers have never experienced anything like the following example.

Look at Figure 1. This data is from a distribution center where the manager was interested in *reducing lost cartons*. A lost carton was one that went to the wrong location in the center. Losing a carton meant that it would not be loaded on the scheduled truck, and when found would have to be shipped later. This resulted in the items not being available in the retail store for timely sale. As you can see from the graph, the center averaged 550 lost cartons per week. While this is only a small percentage of the more than 800,000 cartons shipped every week, it was significant enough to solve. The manager did what most managers do. He set an improvement goal that was pretty aggressive, asking for an improvement of over 10 percent the first week. He then set a linear goal to less than 100 lost cartons seven weeks later. The results show that in the first week after the goal was communicated, lost cartons dropped to only 81. Understand that the manager would have been happy with 490 and ecstatic with 480. No manager in his right mind would have set a stretch goal of 81 for the first week. It is apparent that the goal the manager set had nothing to do with his crew's performance. They did as well as the system would allow from the very first week. This kind of performance can only happen when goals are used in conjunction with feedback on performance (which he provided) to increase positive reinforcement (which he also provided many times a day). Stretch goals limit positive reinforcement for improved performance.

Figure 1

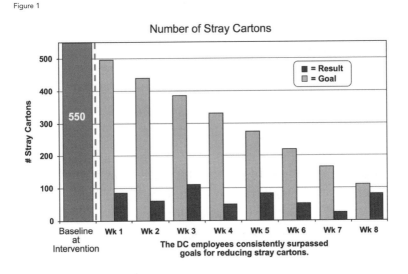

Number of Stray Cartons

The DC employees consistently surpassed goals for reducing stray cartons.

 ## WHAT TO DO INSTEAD

(How to Make Goals Work for You)

Goals are useful in management if they have a clear, logical, and frequent connection to positive reinforcement for productive employee behavior. This can be accomplished in three ways.

1. SET MANY MINI-GOALS

Contrary to popular opinion, the best mistake in setting a

goal is to set it too low. By setting it low you increase the probability of success. By rewarding goal attainment you increase the motivation and achieve subsequent goals. While small incremental goals appear to take longer to produce significant results, the opposite is true. This is because positive reinforcement accelerates performance and small goals provide more opportunities for acceleration.

The knowledgeable manager may find herself in a position where she has to reduce goals performers set, since it is the manager's job to create the conditions for success. If she realizes that the goal is likely to produce failure, she should set the initial goal at a lower level. Success breeds success.

2. MAKE PROGRESS VISIBLE

Display data on a graph so that employees can see progress daily, when possible. If the data is not available daily, use the shortest interval that is possible. Hourly is better than daily. Daily is better than weekly. Weekly is better than monthly. Less than monthly is a waste of time. Look at Figure 2 (Abernathy 2000). Can you tell which companies gave monthly vs. quarterly feedback on performance? Of course, B, C, and F gave feedback quarterly and the others gave it monthly.

3. PLAN POSITIVE REINFORCEMENT FOR IMPROVEMENT

Specific measurable goals combined with frequent feedback and positive reinforcement for improvement form a powerful combination for improvement in the organization. Stajkovic and Luthans (1997) found that goals combined with feedback resulted in 10 percent improvement. Social recognition produced a 17 percent improvement and monetary incentives improved task performance by 23 percent. Combining feedback with social and monetary reinforcement resulted in a 45

Figure 2

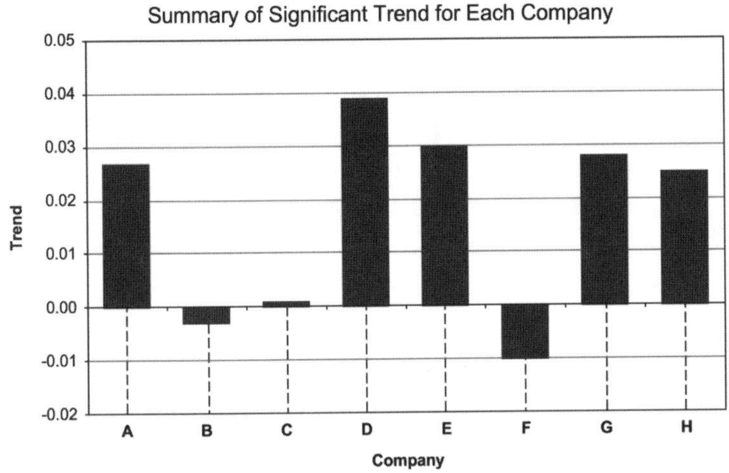
Summary of Significant Trend for Each Company
0.05
0.04
0.03
0.02
0.01
0.00
-0.01
-0.02
Trend
A
B
C
D
E
F
G
H
Company

percent improvement. We have personally witnessed this effect thousands of times over the last 30 years. Improvement of two to three times baseline levels is not uncommon when graphic feedback and effective positive reinforcers have been used.

OBJECTIONS

You might object that stretch goals cannot be all that bad because some studies associate them with good outcomes. However, I believe that when you understand behavior, the studies that show positive results do so because the researchers combined some of the characteristics of good goal-setting that typically are absent from stretch goals. Here is how I interpret the research findings:

1. **Schulz et al. (2006) state, "A central finding of the goal-setting literature is that specific, difficult**

goals lead to better performance than no goals, or do-your-best goals." From a behavioral perspective, this makes sense because many things become possible when goals specify desired outcomes. Employees know exactly what is expected of them. Progress toward the goal is easily tracked (e.g., through graphic feedback) and positive reinforcement can be provided for goal-related behaviors. Very little of this is possible with no goals or do-your-best goals.

2. **Tiered stretch goals, a recent innovation in the research, are more effective than non-tiered ones** (Bateman and Ludwig, 2003). With tiered-stretch goal research, employees are usually put into two or more groups and the stretch goals are set from the average performance of the groups. Tiered goals may work better than non-tiered goals simply because they are likely to be more realistic. Since they have some obvious connection to actual past employee performance, it is logical that they may be met more readily.

3. **The second iteration of stretch goals (whether traditional or tiered) typically produces a deterioration of performance, particularly when the goals are increased (ratcheted)** (Schulz et al., 2006). Because tiered stretch goals are based on the average performance of multiple groups, it is likely that many employees do not meet these either. Deterioration in performance is expected after employees fail to reach the goals because positive reinforcement is absent. Even when employees reach the first stretch goal, it has to be somewhat daunting to face

the prospect of yet another low-probability goal.

4. **Goals that enhance performer self-efficacy are most likely to be achieved** (Lee et al., 1997) (Bandura, 1994). Self-efficacy is a prominent concept in goal setting research. It usually is defined as the extent to which the performer believes he can achieve the goal. One can tap into roughly the same thing without having to get inside employees' heads by simply measuring the performer's success or failure rate in past attempts. Those who have had a lot of success in reaching goals are more likely to believe they can achieve a difficult goal than those who have failed in past attempts. It is obvious that few people have a history of success with stretch goals as they are defined as low-probability events. Therefore, self-efficacy would be low in most stretch goal practices.

5. **Stretch goals are more successful when employee commitment is present than when it is missing** (Hollenbeck and Klein, 1987). Here, *commitment* is defined as the attractiveness of the goal to the performers. Yet goals are attractive to the extent that they are (a) attainable and (b) associated with a positive reinforcer or reward for goal attainment. Why would employees not get more excited about goals when reinforcers and rewards are available than when none exist? In all of the research, employees performed better when there were social or tangible (monetary or items of value) reinforcers for goal attainment. Goals are never attractive as an end unto themselves; they are attractive as a means to an end.

In short, when success follows stretch goals, it is because they have been combined with features that make sense within a science of behavior. None of the above, however, means that stretch goals are a good idea. Even better-performing stretch goal systems are unlikely to outshine goal systems designed to deliver positive reinforcement for the smallest improvement.

GOALS VERSUS THE NEED FOR INNOVATION AND CREATIVITY

Goal setting is appropriate if: 1) You are not where you need to be, but know that the goal has been reached in the past; 2) you are performing below your competitors who have the same basic processes and equipment; 3) you are performing at or ahead of your competitors but know improvement is possible.

Goal setting primarily involves behavior shaping—the process of positively reinforcing successive approximations (or small steps) toward a goal. The improvement often comes, not only from increasing the rate of behavior but also by spending more time involved in goal-related activity.

If employees are working as hard as they can and cannot reach the desired or necessary performance level, creativity is required. This means that doing the old things more efficiently or effectively will *not* solve the problem. *Creativity* is, by definition, "out-of-the-box-thinking" and often involves a radical departure from an existing process. For example, the Fair Tax (Boortz and Linder, 2006) is a creative solution to the problem of funding the government. Adjusting tax rates is an attempt to make the existing form of funding the government more effective and efficient.

A thesis of this book, however, is that managerial habits are often deeply engrained. The same is true of employee habits. In order for a creative process to emerge, it is necessary for the current approaches to undergo extinction. Solutions that involve tweaking the current process must be rejected, and it is up to managers to establish a context in which alternatives are vigorously examined.

Many attempts at creativity and innovation have been abandoned when a breakthrough was imminent because the managers did not understand the behavior patterns characteristic of extinction (for details, see Daniels, 2002).

In the vernacular, creativity means *working smarter.* Getting people to work smarter requires lots of reinforcement initially, not for results, but for generating new ideas. It also requires managers to have a high tolerance for failure. Most new ideas don't work, but punishing ideas that don't work also punishes idea generation. To learn more about behavioral approaches to promoting creativity, read Epstein (1990) and Daniels (2000).

To summarize, stretch goals are commonly used, but this does not mean that they are effective. Incremental goals combined with graphic feedback and frequent positive reinforcement not only produce better and faster results, but also create an environment in which people will enjoy accomplishing them. What more could you ask?

o   o   o   o   o   o

#3
PERFORMANCE APPRAISAL

"By only infrequently rating personnel
we only infrequently demotivate them."
–*Blogger, 2008*

I have said often, and only somewhat facetiously, that the best way to double the effectiveness of the typical annual performance appraisal is to do it once every two years. No activity in corporate life is more universally despised, by both managers and employees, than performance appraisal. The person giving the appraisal faces a no-win situation because if the appraisal is good, the performer expected it; but if it is negative, a bad scene might ensue.

Several studies show that 80 percent of employees think they perform in the top 20 percent of the employee population. This means that at least 60 percent of employees, at any given time, are unhappy about their performance rating. So why do we put ourselves through it? Is it some sadistic ritual? Susan Heathfield, a writer for *About.com,* describes it succinctly when she writes, "Employee performance appraisal is painful and it doesn't work."

A 1994 survey by the Society for Human Resource Management (SHRM) found that 90 percent of appraisal systems were not successful (Shellhardt, 1994). I can't imagine that they are any more successful today. After all, companies have been tweaking the appraisal process for over 50 years to no avail. Rating schemes have changed. Competencies have appeared. Pay (supposedly) has been separated from the appraisal process. The number of raters has been increased. All these many changes have not made the process any more desirable or effective.

Coens and Jenkins (2000), for example, call these changes "appraisal with novel packaging." One of the novel packagings is to call this activity *performance management* rather than *performance appraisal.* I have used the term *performance management* to describe the application of behavior analysis research to the management of organizational performance, which is detailed in the book, *Performance Management: Changing Behavior that Drives Organizational Effectiveness* (Daniels and Daniels, 2002). In that book, the term *performance management* includes appraisal but focuses on how people are managed day-to-day and how policies, processes, and procedures support people on the frontline of the organization. So when you see this term in different contexts, make sure you understand the way it is being used because usually it is not being applied according to my definition.

Some of the other names for performance appraisal currently in vogue are stack ranking, 360° feedback, and performance review. But as we all know, if it looks like a duck . . . Performance appraisal by any other name is still performance appraisal. Changing the name doesn't change a flawed process. How is the performance appraisal process flawed?

PERFORMANCE APPRAISAL IS A PUNISHING PROCESS

The performance appraisal process is punishing to the rater and the ratee. I have never known a manager who looked forward to performance review sessions. Since 80 percent of employees think they perform in the top 20 percent of the employee population, most employees receive a rating lower than they think is accurate, a punishing experience. Because punishment decreases behavior, the result of the performance appraisal session for most people is to decrease motivation. It is a common problem that supervisors and managers do not complete the appraisals in a timely manner. Sometimes, if HR does not follow up consistently, years may go by with no appraisal in the file. Why would you not put off a process that is punishing, if you could get away with it? Why do organizations continue to have a process that no one likes? There must be a better way.

PERFORMANCE APPRAISAL *PRODUCES* A LOW PERCENTAGE OF TOP PERFORMERS

With the exception of the Federal Government which is forbidden by law to have quotas, almost all organizations have some sort of forced distribution appraisal model. Whether formally or informally stated, most organizations have an understanding about the percentage of employees that can be given a top performance rating. This creates what has been referred to as a zero-sum game in that when the top category is filled, everyone else will receive a lower rating. This kind of system certainly does not enhance teamwork and has been known to create unhealthy competition among employees.

The assumption behind forced distributions is that if you take a random sample of people and rate them on almost any personal characteristic, from height to intelligence, people will fall out in what is called a normal distribution with 99 percent of the sample falling within three standard deviations of the mean. In other words while most people will cluster around some average intellectual ability, a few will be very smart and a few will demonstrate limited intellectual ability. Most business people know this as the *bell curve* since the distribution of scores has a bell shape.

Human resources has used this statistical model as justification for using a forced distribution appraisal system. The problem is that companies don't hire a random sample of the population. No one has ever gone to HR and said, "We have so many smart people that we have to hire some dummies to get to a normal distribution." Today, many organizations use a distribution that is skewed toward the higher scores. That is, a preponderance of employees will fall into the two top rating groups in a five-group system. Even at that, they are forcing a distribution on who they thought at hiring to be highly motivated, smart people. In essence, organizations spend time and effort recruiting and hiring the best of the best, then (through forced distribution assessment systems) they proceed to tell most employees that they don't measure up to the company's standards for reward. It simply doesn't make sense!

Many people who attend my seminars assert that they don't have a required distribution for rating performance. My questions to these people are, *What would happen if you gave all your people the top rating?* or *Has any supervisor set a performance objective to have all employees rated in the top performance category?* I have never understood how an organization can remain competitive in a global economy when a mere 10 to 20 percent of its employees are outstanding performers. Why wouldn't a company strive for an entire workforce of outstanding employees? How many customers want an organization's mediocre employees to build their products or provide their services?

It is certainly possible to have an organization where everyone performs at the highest level. Yet, while many managers would not like it if a large percentage of employees were ranked in the top category (meaning higher pay raises), few managers would be upset with a supervisor if fewer than expected were given the top rating. Somewhere along the line, the primary reason for performance assessment (to help people improve performance) has been forgotten.

> The person who has had more impact on the appraisal process than any other in the last 50 years is Jack Welch of GE fame. He introduced a process that has been sarcastically called *rank-and-yank*. In a letter to shareholders at GE he wrote, "A company that bets its future on its people must remove that lower 10 percent, and keep removing it every year—always raising the bar of performance and increasing the quality of its leadership." Jack Welch did a lot of things right in his many years as the chief executive of GE but this cannot be considered his finest hour.

Unfortunately, because of the way Welch is idolized by many executives, a large number of organizations copied this model, not always with great success. The practice has led to numerous employee lawsuits costing companies millions of dollars. Welch could not have thought through the implications of his statement. What does such a practice do to morale, teamwork, and voluntary turnover? From a behavioral perspective, this approach is doomed to have a devastating impact on morale, teamwork, and ultimately performance. It produces an environment where employees compete with each other more than with competitors in the marketplace.

Welch said that his rank-and-yank process was necessary because managers and supervisors will not make difficult decisions about poor performers. While some managers and supervisors might not make the difficult decision of firing someone, creating a system that forces managers to fire a certain number of employees every year is hardly the answer. If you are hiring competent people, what does it say about an organization when 10 percent of those people fail each year? What is the cost in terms of morale, teamwork, voluntary turnover, and eventually the company's viability? What does this practice do to the employee's perception of their leaders? What compromises are made around the issue of values?

During a seminar break, a man approached me and asked if I was a psychologist. I responded that I used to be. He said, "My boss is a huge fan of Jack Welch and we have to give 10 percent of our employees a three rating each year, which is the lowest rating. If a person receives a three rating two years in a row, he is fired. Since you were a psychologist, I would love to have you come and watch my people work. I have 30 in my department and I don't believe you would be able to tell which should get a three. They are all great. I know everybody probably says that about their employees, so I would love to have you watch them and give me your opinion. However, I have figured a way out of my problem, but I don't like to have to do it. I rotate the people who get a three so that no one gets that rating for two years in a row."

Another manager solved this problem in a different way by having employees draw their rating out of a hat! While it may be difficult for many executives to believe that the system could be perverted in this way, I have heard numerous stories of similar ways for dealing with a bad system.

While grading on the curve may have been introduced as a way to force supervisors and managers to make the difficult decisions, these examples indicate that it has not been entirely successful . . . to say the least.

Most people who take a job really want to do that job to the best of their ability. If someone ends up not doing a good job, management should ask what it has done, or not done, that might have contributed to the poor performance. This should be the first question asked in order to help the person improve. The ultimate responsibility for motivation lies with management, not with the employee. It is management's responsibility to create a workplace that causes employees to do their best every day. Policies, procedures, processes, equipment, and management behavior can either cause people to do their best or to do just enough to get by.

IT'S NOT ABOUT THE MONEY

Some organizations seem to think that separating issues of pay from the appraisal process makes it more effective. While it solves none of the problems above, it does eliminate some contentious conversation from the appraisal session. However, it would be a dense employee indeed who would not understand that even though pay is not mentioned in the appraisal session, it is related to performance in some way. Separating pay raises and appraisal discussions simply delays the contentious conversation. Not mentioning money is at best *the elephant in the room* that will stick around long after the session is over. It is a ruse for management to pretend that appraisal and compensation are unrelated because even the most poorly run organizations attempt to correlate pay with performance. When pay is unrelated to performance, it puts the organization at risk.

PERFORMANCE RATING CATEGORIES ARE POORLY DEFINED BEHAVIORALLY

It is almost impossible for anyone to watch employees work and accurately determine who falls into which rating category. The differences in behavior between those in the bottom of the top category and the top of the next one are so small that it is impossible to reliably separate them by what they do and what they produce even when you do extensive work sampling.

W. Edwards Deming, quality pioneer, attempted to solve this problem by limiting the appraisal categories to three, separated by standard deviations. His intention was to make sure that the categories separated employees into groups that were significantly different in performance. While this solved the problem of making sure there were real differences between categories, it did nothing to change the basic assumptions behind the need to appraise in the first place. It is not the number of categories or how they are separated that makes the performance appraisal process problematic; it is the faulty assumptions upon which the entire activity is based.

We worked, for example, with a national company some years ago that hired the best engineers money could buy. They wanted only the top students from the top engineering schools in the country and often got them. However, the unwritten rule was that new employees could only get a three rating in a five rating system. How motivating is that to a young person who has worked day and night to show the new employer that he or she has what it takes to be successful? A three is a C to these people and they have probably never made a C in their entire academic careers. I predicted that the most likely outcome of this process was that these engineers would either quit and leave the company or they would quit and stay with the company. They quickly learned one thing for sure: success is not determined by what you do, but what you do relative to all the others, maybe. Only a quota system could create such a demotivating practice.

PERFORMANCE APPRAISAL IS A MANAGER BEHAVIOR

Another complication in the process is that performance appraisal is a manager behavior, not an employee behavior. Because the employee is rated on traits, competencies, and other less-than-objective variables, the rater can hardly avoid having a personal influence on the outcome.

Look at these performance standards from an eight-page

performance appraisal form currently in use:

- Makes decisions and takes actions that demonstrate organizational awareness
- Makes substantive contributions when working on teams
- Acquires new skills and knowledge through traditional and other means
- Demonstrates ethics, integrity, and accountability

Every manager is familiar with this kind of evaluation. Such actions and activities are rarely measured in a consistent and objective way. Therefore, manager bias always exists in the ratings, opening the process up to many complaints and much dissatisfaction.

WHY DO WE CONTINUE TO DO IT?

Generally speaking, organizations conduct performance appraisals for five reasons: employee development, employee motivation, promotion, pay, and for legal termination. However, none of these reasons are satisfied or accomplished when the data are carefully scrutinized. Let's consider them.

1. **Employee development**. Often the same items appear in the employee's development section, year after year. From what is known about behavior, it is very unlikely that substantial improvement can be made with only one or even four opportunities for performance feedback in a year's time.

2. **Employee motivation.** While the top 20 percent may be motivated to do better and that is not a certainty, 80 percent are bound to be unhappy and demotivated.

3. **Promotion.** Since over half of all leaders fail, (Daniels and Daniels, 2005), this cannot be an effective criterion for choosing a leader, manager, or supervisor.

4. **Pay.** Since pay is separated from the process, there must be other criteria that are more important in making pay decisions.

5. **Legal termination.** Data indicates that in 44 percent of the cases performance appraisals actually favor the plaintiff's case in the courts and seven out of 10 attorneys surveyed state that appraisals don't give the company an advantage in litigation (Coens and Jenkins, 2000).

WHAT TO DO INSTEAD

While most managers personally experience all the problems of performance appraisal mentioned, they feel that it is still necessary because a better alternative isn't available. Actually, there are better alternatives. In order to understand what they are, you must first answer the question, "What are you trying to accomplish?" If you are trying to create an organization where people do their best every day, the annual performance appraisal will play a minor role, if any, and almost always interferes with that goal.

In the final analysis, if all employees did outstanding work every day there would be no need for an appraisal system as we know it. Therefore, it seems that what organizations need is the knowledge, systems, and management practices to create such an organization, because it is possible.

Some people think that you can make the performance

appraisal work better by doing it more often. That is partially true. However, using a bad process more often doesn't make it better. If the information energizes the performer and causes him to improve work performance, more is better; if not, less is better.

I have often said, "The best job you will ever have is one in which you know how well you have done at the end of every working day." Knowledge of how you are doing is essential to any kind of improvement. The best feedback cycle is immediate. The longer the interval between feedback opportunities, the fewer opportunities there are for improvement. When employees know how they are doing at every moment in time, performance is highest. Of course, this requires job measurement and positive reinforcement for improvement.

It is a common management belief that many of the jobs in today's workplace can't be measured. Every job can be measured and performers will help you measure them when they learn that measurement is used to help them perform better and not used as the basis for criticism and punishment.

We have used a performance matrix[1] to measure jobs from the frontline to the executive suite. See Daniels and Daniels (2002) for a more detailed explanation. Performers develop their matrices with their supervisor and track their performance during the month. This way, employees know at every point in time how well they are doing. Combined with the frequent delivery of positive reinforcement for improvement, the two create a powerful motivational force that will eliminate the need for performance appraisal as we currently know it.

[1] A copy of a Performance Matrix is included in the Appendix.

The goal of this type of appraisal should be to have all employees performing in the top group. Rewards for managers should be contingent on the number of performers reaching the top level, not on some aggregate measure of the unit performance. When manager success is determined by employee success it changes the behavior of the manager from evaluator to coach. This creates much more involvement in the day-to-day performance of employees.

In a company I visited in Japan a number of years ago, a manager who recommended someone for a supervisory or managerial position followed the person's achievement since the person's success or failure was a reflection on the recommending manager. This ensured that the manager would do everything he/she could to make the new manager successful. Creating new leaders is a major responsibility of every supervisor.

Managers and supervisors should be teachers and coaches who do not sit in judgment of employees but as those who transfer their knowledge and experience to others in an efficient and positive manner. The evaluation of the manager should be not only on whether employees succeed but also on the manager behaviors used to help them achieve success.

o   o   o   o   o   o

#4
RANKING

You don't have to do your best,
just better than the one in second place.

–Aubrey Daniels

Where there are objective measures of performance, a regular practice is to use various sources of sales, accounting, and productivity/quality data to rank employees, stores, plants, and offices. It is very common to rank salespeople and to publish the rankings publicly. If such information is not posted on the wall for all to see, it is sent in an e-mail or included in a monthly report to the sales force. The thinking behind this practice is that the ranking will motivate the ones on the bottom to improve and possibly create even higher performance by the others.

One of the problems with this practice is that, even if sales go down or plant or office performance declines, there is still someone at the top and someone at the bottom. It is possible that the person or people at the top do not have to do his/their best but only do enough to be better than the closest competitor. As the story goes, you don't have to out-run the bear, you just have to outrun the person behind you.

COMPETITION–TAKE IT OUTSIDE

A more serious problem is that ranking inhibits sharing and promotes unhealthy competition. Jim, a senior V.P. of a major manufacturing company, took over as general manager of a division that had seven regional service centers. He was known as a tough manager. These regional service centers performed the same service, were organized similarly, and were ranked monthly on overall performance.

Shortly after taking over, Jim made a visit to all the plants. When in Atlanta, he discovered that the Atlanta center was still struggling with a problem that Dallas had solved months ago. Jim immediately called the Dallas manager to find out why he had not told the Atlanta manager what he had done to correct the problem. The manager said he "was pretty sure" that he had told the Atlanta center manager what they had done. When I tell you that the Dallas center ranked sixth and the Atlanta center ranked seventh, do you think the Dallas manager really thought he had talked to the Atlanta manager?

In a similar situation when a new manager, Russ, came on the scene, his reputation preceded him. He was known to make quick and frequent management changes when performance did not meet his expectations. At the end of Russ' first month on the job, the plant that was consistently ranked last went from last place to the middle of the pack. At the end of the second month, this plant went from the middle of the pack to number two and remained there the following month. Russ became suspicious. He went to the plant and spent the day observing the operation. At the end of the day he confronted the plant manager by asking, "Where did you get these numbers?" The manager looked at the floor and said quietly, "I made them up." Russ could hardly believe what he heard. "Why did you make them up?" The reply was simple, "I got tired of being at the bottom." Of course Russ fired him, as he should, since dishonesty is a show stopper. However, the system produced this kind of behavior. Such a system encourages people to shade the results, if not outright lie, and causes them to hold back on sharing improvements. Certainly it does not pay to share when the rankings create mostly negative consequences for a majority of the performers.

In another example, a large regional bank in the Southeast ranked branches on performance. They stopped the practice when managers discovered that employees were reluctant to spend time servicing customers from other branches and even referred them back to their own branches.

Competition between employees, departments, plants, and offices is more destructive than motivational. It encourages people to take shortcuts, take financial and safety risks, skip steps related to quality, and save results for the next reporting period when you don't have a chance at being number one in the present month.

Your competition is not inside your organization; employees should be competing with your real competitors, not with each other. To the extent that people are motivated by this practice, the motivation is toward unhealthy competition rather than cooperation and sharing.

WHAT TO DO INSTEAD

Eliminate ranking for motivational purposes. It may be helpful in making decisions relative to promotions and assignments but it does not motivate teams or individuals.

External benchmarking is a good way to motivate individuals and groups. Benchmarks allow you to compete with a real competitor or someone who is best in class for what you do. Beating the competition, closing the gap between you and the benchmark, and *becoming* the benchmark are all highly motivating.

Another way to motivate units or individuals is to use goals in the manner described in the section on stretch goals. Set a target of improving on past performance or toward some performance criterion. Set individual goals for each unit or person. Report on the number who meet or exceed their target. You could even list the names of the individuals or units above goal, but list the names alphabetically, not by performance. As people or units get above goal, you may want to add other levels, such as silver, gold, and platinum. The key is that you don't limit the number of units or performers in any of the categories. You would, of course, want everyone or every unit to be in the highest category. The environment you should create is one where people help each other. If I am in the platinum category and you are in the gold, there should be no reason that I would not want to help you reach the platinum level as well. By helping you, I would at least get social reinforcement from you for the help and you would be more likely to share your ideas and help me in the future.

A way to encourage cooperation is to add a reward for group accomplishment over and above the individual reinforcement. For example, you might set goals for each individual, department, store, or office and plan some reinforcement or rewards for that accomplishment but add an additional reward if all individuals in the group meet their targets.

I'd like to share a story from long ago that really made an impression on me about how a properly designed work or school environment can be created where individual success increases the probability of the success of others.

A friend of mine, a university psychology professor, designed a course in which he determined what a student should know on finishing the course. He developed 20 units of study and three quizzes for each unit. To move from one unit to another, the student had to pass a quiz on the unit with a score of 100. If he did not, the professor would give additional assignments for the problem areas and retest until the student learned the material to the criterion. Students completing 19-20 units successfully got an A. Completing 17-18 resulted in a B and 15-16 got a C. If you considered yourself a C student, you could complete 15 units and the course would be over for you.

He said it didn't surprise him when by mid-semester over half of the class finished with an A. (Of course it surprised the Dean. Have you ever wondered why the symbol of academic excellence is in such short supply? If an A meant the student mastered the course, why would a teacher not want all the students to earn one? Why would a teacher think he/she had transferred knowledge successfully if most students mastered less than 70 percent of the material? Well, that is another story for another occasion. Don't get me started.) My friend was surprised, however, that over half of the students who got an A continued to come to class even when they had already earned the top grade. Why did they come to class when they didn't have to? To help the other students get an A.

When the conditions are right, people will not only achieve at high rates, but will assist others in doing the same. Think of the possibility of an organization where *everyone* is your best student or employee.

o   o   o   o   o   o

#5
REWARDING THINGS A
DEAD MAN CAN DO

If a dead man can do it perfectly, it won't solve your problem.
–Ogden Lindsley

On the face of it, rewarding things a dead man, or woman, can do sounds crazy. Of course, it makes no sense to reward employees for something a dead person could do but it is done in corporations every day. Have no accidents, make no errors, and be at your workstation or desk are three of the more common ones. While I understand that no organization wants defects or accidents, (or dead people in workstations), believe it or not, you really don't want to manage to those goals. If you reward employees for zero defects, the sure way to do that is to make no product. While that may seem absurd, rewarding a department for having zero defects in a given period might not cause the employees to do nothing (due to other on-the-job requirements) but it will in all likelihood affect production in a negative way. Because of all the hoopla promoting zero defects as a necessity for organizations' survival, the consequences to employees for producing a defect may be more personal, and negative, than those for decreasing production.

In celebrating millions of hours without a lost-time accident, you can bet as the organization approaches the milestone, performance will be negatively impacted as no one wants to be the person to have an accident. Therefore, employees are careful to a fault. Dead men have no accidents. Rewarding and celebrating no accidents and no defects may result in hiding defects or even not reporting minor accidents.

We worked in a paper mill in south Alabama a number of years ago where the plant manager expected managers and supervisors to be in the plant when he arrived and be in the plant when he left the plant. Can a dead man spend long hours in the plant? I assure you that very little work was done as they waited on the plant manager to leave at the end of the day. He engendered a great deal of ill will, and very little additional performance, by his expectation that managers spend long hours in the plant. In a similar vein, the president of a software development company, behind in their product releases, counted the cars in the parking lot when he left at 5 o'clock on Friday. If the number did not meet his expectations, the VP of R&D was in for a difficult Monday.

DO SOMETHING! ESPECIALLY IF IT'S RIGHT

We hire people to do things that increase value, not to stop something. We want employees to work safely 100 percent of the time. We want employees to produce defect-free products at an increasing rate. We want software developers to write effective code, solve complex problems, and complete projects. Don't argue; don't interrupt; be at your workstation, don't take long breaks: all of these pass the Dead Man's Test.[2]

Some think the Dead Man's Test amounts to a trivial discrimination and is just a play on words. The reality is that the test causes you to focus on very different things. All the president can do after finding few cars in the parking lot is to chew out the VP and demand that people put in the hours or else. The problem is that, even if the number of cars increase, there is no guarantee that project quality or completion will be improved or even that the people, rather than their cars, are at the office. In fact, what the president didn't know was that most of the software engineers left early to spend a few hours at home before returning to the office and working most of the night. If you were one of these software engineers who worked late, how would you react to the president's demand? It shouldn't surprise you to learn that the division continued to be late with their product deliveries and that the president was replaced several months later.

In safety if you are working on increasing hours without a lost-time accident (a dead man violation), you focus on safety almost to the exclusion of productivity. However, if you are trying to increase safe working behavior, you kill two birds with one stone, no pun intended. If you are trying to have a

---

[2] Dr. Ogden Lindsley, longtime professor at the University of Kansas, and a pioneer in the field of behavior analysis, came up with the Dead Man's Test. He defined *dead man behavior* as, "If a dead man can do it perfectly, it won't solve your problem." If a behavior passes the Dead Man's Test, you have pinpointed the wrong behavior.

million hours without a lost time accident, you may find your-self splitting hairs as to whether something will qualify as an accident. A maintenance department supervisor may assign work that is inherently safe and put off the work that has a higher risk till after the goal has been met. As it relates to quality, when rewards for zero defects hang in the balance, defective product will not be counted or it may be placed in a corner or taken out of the plant or office under someone's coat because the consequences in such a situation are more severe for producing a defect than missing a production goal.

ACCOMPLISHMENT ACCOUNTABILITY

Although it may not seem that a cost of living allowance is a dead man violation, on closer inspection it is. Anytime you do anything across the board it has the effect of rewarding some employees for dead man behavior. While a company that offers good benefits and compensation may attract good peo-ple, these things create no guarantee of high performance. If high wages and benefits guaranteed high performance, the American auto industry would have the highest performance in the world since, for a long time, they had the highest wages and benefits of any industry.

I believe that when Henry Ford unilaterally increased the wages of his employees to $5 a day, he started a practice that has ultimately led to the deterioration of the industry, one in which wages are determined by being on the payroll rather than by accomplishment. It worked for Henry because the increase went to employees who as a group were largely hardworking immigrants. The problem was created when succeeding generations got the increases, whether they were hardworking or not, and indeed saw them as entitlements.

Most employees today expect their companies to guarantee that wages and benefits keep pace with the cost of living. This practice began in England when in 1795 magistrates began supplementing wages to the poor based on the price of a loaf of bread and the number of children in the family. This practice did not reduce the number of poor in England and may very well have increased that number.

Increasing wages and benefits because of inflation does not increase value for the organization and in the long run is detrimental for the employees. It is a practice that is harmful to the economic health of the company and works an insidious effect on the morale and performance of the organization. High performing companies can get away with this practice since the increases in compensation and benefits generally fall on efficient and effective behavior. The problem comes when performance drops and the practice continues. Even though you probably would not have dead people on the payroll, some may perform as though they are on life support. Whether employees are hardworking, hardly working, or not working at all, they get the same increases in benefits and at times, even compensation.

WHO BENEFITS?

A considerable body of evidence showing that any time you give any form of reward—money, benefits, perks, and so on—independent of performance, you dilute the effectiveness of the *earned* rewards and ultimately teach employees to be dependent on the largess of the company. While a cost of living allowance is rarely rejected, it causes a change in behavior that is seen only over the long haul. Each incident of non-contingent reinforcement is a plank in the house of entitlement.

[Each incident of positive reinforcement given independent of performance is referred to as *non-contingent.*]

When morale is poor, it is a waste of time and money to improve benefits or increase compensation. Remember, reinforcement increases or strengthens the behavior that is occurring when you get it. Your intended target for improvement does not matter; your reinforcement will increase the behavior that is happening when the reinforcement is delivered. In a poor morale situation, talking negatively about management and the company is a dominant behavior. Deliver even a well-intentioned, non-contingent reinforcer in the face of poor morale and you will get more of that negative behavior.

As I mentioned earlier, I believe that compensation and benefits should be as high as profits will allow. Nothing in this book is designed to reduce money in employees' pockets, just the opposite. If an executive knows that for every dollar she puts in an employee's pocket, the company will get $10 in return, what executive would not want to pay people more? But it is not a matter of whether to give employees money, benefits, and other perks; rather it is a matter of who to give it to and why. Obviously the people who work the hardest and produce the most should get the most.

Any time you deliver positive reinforcers or rewards to everyone across the board, you displease the hardest working employees the most because they begin to ask themselves why they should work so hard when everyone receives the same payoff. This is not a good strategy. While it is administratively easy, it is costly in terms of performance and morale.

Admittedly, companies today must offer a range of benefits to attract employees. To the extent that a company provides benefits and understands that it is a cost of doing business, I have no argument. However, many companies increase benefits under the assumption that there will be an increase in performance or at least in loyalty that will offset the cost of the benefit. They are almost always disappointed.

WHAT TO DO INSTEAD

There is a proverb that says, "Praise makes good people better and bad people worse." You must be careful what you reinforce because you are sure to get more of it. Years ago I was talking to a supervisor in a manufacturing plant in Minnesota about a problem employee. He complained, "I'm not paying him to loaf all day; I'm paying him to do a job." I asked, "Is he getting paid?" "Yes," he replied. "Is he doing his job?" "No." "Is he loafing all day?" "Yes," he repeated. "Then he is getting paid to loaf." I said.

1. **Make sure that reinforcement, recognition, and reward are earned.** The antidote to eliminating dead man behavior is to make sure that the perks, benefits, and compensation are directly related to the contribution of employees. Check policies, procedures, and processes to make sure that dead man behaviors are identified and eliminated. Replace them with the behavior you want rather than the behavior you don't want. Any time you are trying to reduce something, you run the risk of committing a dead man violation. Determine what you want and reinforce it, recognize it, reward it, and pay for it. Think *earn*. Earning is active. When people earn, they are confident and competent. Non-contingent reinforcement creates dependency.

Executives I talk to all over the country are concerned about an increasing entitlement mentality. How do you create an entitlement mentality? You give people what they want and ask nothing of them. A friend of mine says that a weekly allowance is a child's first lesson in entitlement. A weekly allowance is like a salary. The connection between the child's behavior and the payout of such an allowance is often weak. A chore-based allowance (performance-based pay) is more preferred because there is a clear connection between the child's behavior and the money.

2. **Know whose behavior created a result.** Before giving any reinforcement, recognition, or reward, ask the question, "What did the person do to earn it?" Just being on the payroll passes the Dead Man's Test. Could the result have been accomplished if this person did nothing? Looking only at results will never tell you that you have dead man behavior in the performance chain. When recognizing or rewarding someone, you should always know how results were obtained. Frequently, business results are obtained by someone other than the one who takes the credit. Make sure that a result was not obtained by someone else having to step in and complete the work that others should have done. When you look only at results, you will never see who accomplished a task or how they did it. Knowledge of both is critical for building an organization that creates the highest value.

o   o   o   o   o   o

#6
SALARY AND HOURLY PAY
(to include annual raises and bonuses)

Money is a beautifully honed instrument for recognizing and creating worthy performance. It is the principal tool for supplying incentives for competence and therefore deserves great respect. Any frivolous use of money weakens its power to promote human capital—the true wealth of nations.

—Thomas Gilbert

The modern organization wastes more time and money in the way people are compensated than it wastes in any other area of the business. Salary and hourly pay is pay for showing up, not for performing. Raises are forever. Bonuses are only loosely contingent on performance. Even profit sharing and pay-for-performance plans are poorly designed to create the best performance.

In almost every study of various methods of pay, salary and hourly pay produce the lowest performance. Behavior analysis calls these pay plans a *fixed-time schedule* of reinforcement. This simply means that pay is contingent on the passage of some interval of time, not what one does in that time. Whether employees do outstanding work or goof off, they will get a paycheck at the end of the week or month as long as they are on the payroll. Because people are paid for showing up, other motivational schemes, supervisory and monetary, are needed to ensure that performance is at least equal to the pay. Indeed, Abernathy (2000) makes the case that if compensation is properly structured, you can essentially create a self-managed workforce which dramatically reduces the cost of supervision for both hourly and salaried performers.

RAISES: AN EXPENSIVE USE OF MONEY

There are at least two problems with raises. The first and most serious is that a $1000 raise is worth tens of thousands of dollars when compounded over the employment lifetime. If management could count on an increase in performance equal to the investment over the years, this wouldn't be a problem; but with the way raises are given, that is often not the case. The investment may be good for some individuals, but overall the return on a raise is poor. I am sure that the vast majority of managers would agree.

Another problem with raises is that they are rarely motivational. Once you have the raise, the increase becomes an entitlement; no one will take it away because pay is rarely reduced due to poor performance. If making a large salary were motivational, there would never be performance issues with highly paid managers and executives. Everyone knows that is not the case.

Believe it or not, because of the way raises are distributed they are often punishing rather than reinforcing. In a classic vignette from Robert Mager's film *Who Did What To Whom,* a boss announces to an employee, "and I was able to get you a five percent raise." The woman sitting in front of the desk slams a note pad on the desk and says angrily as she walks out of the office, "You call that a raise!" Although very few employees respond outwardly in that manner, I am sure they would like to do so because over the years I have been told as much by many people. Often, the difference between raises to the top performers and the next category is only one or two percent. You call that a raise! Many don't.

PAY-FOR-PERFORMANCE: AN INEXPENSIVE USE OF MONEY

Since every job holder is paid in expectation of some kind of performance, the best form of pay is pay-for-performance. No one can argue with the basic concept. Whether one is a factory worker, an art teacher, a journalist, or an executive, all are hired to create a valued outcome for the organization. Unfortunately many of the pay-for-performance plans are not truly pay for performance at all and, again, are also a waste of time and money. The concept of pay-for-performance is behaviorally sound but is seldom designed and implemented correctly in most organizations.

The most basic form of pay-for-performance is piece-rate pay where performers are paid by the number of pieces produced. These systems always produce significant results over hourly pay systems. For example, Safelite Glass Corp. saw a 44 percent increase in output when they switched from hourly pay to piece-rate pay (Lazear, 2000).

In the *putting-out* system of manufacturing that preceded the industrial revolution in England, workers were paid for producing products in their homes, but the merchants had difficulty controlling efficient use of the materials that were supplied for manufacturing. Theft of material, quality of the product, and the time it took to produce the product were constant problems. Yet these were not problems with the payment method but of the contingencies of reinforcement that were used. If the merchants had paid only for quality pieces that were produced in a timely manner at an acceptable cost, the method of pay would have consistently produced superior results.

Why haven't more organizations moved to piece-rate, then? The answer is two-fold: 1) not every job is one where the output is pieces and 2) numerous organizations using piece-rate had difficulty with some aspect of performance.

Piece-rate issues are always management issues, not conceptual ones. Creating a job that can't be measured is a management issue. Changing the rate when employees begin to make more than was expected, which is frequently done, is management behavior. Getting higher production at the expense of quality is a design issue.

Sales commission is a form of pay for performance. It is not as effective as piece-rate because the connection between a salesperson's behavior and the result is not as strong as it is in piecework. Companies can make decisions to buy a product based on customer demand, technical performance, cost and other factors that may be unrelated to the behavior of the salesperson. In spite of these problems, commissions outperform salary because commissions are *more* contingent on behavior than salary.

I have heard at least a hundred times that the best salesperson is the poorest at paperwork, employee relations, and sharing with other salespersons. This is not because the form of pay is bad but because the performance contingencies are wrong. If commissions are earned not only for the sale, but when the paperwork is completed, where the relationships with manufacturing and accounting are positive, and where information about the marketplace is shared with other sales-persons, you will get more of all of those things.

When you see the phrase "pay for performance" don't assume that it is referring to a true pay-for-performance plan. Most of the time the phrase refers to some group pay plan, which is not really pay for performance. Pay for performance in most companies means that when there is a group accom-plishment, all the employees in the group are rewarded. If a company does well or if a plant or even department performs above expectations, people receive performance pay. In these plans, what individuals are paid is not based on their own performance but on some aggregate performance of the group. Typically the best performers and the poorest per-formers receive the same amount given the same job. This design only further reduces the connection between perform-ance and pay. It is quite possible, even probable, that a small percentage of employees in a group can carry the group. This is an example of the 80/20 rule: 20 percent of the employees produce 80 percent of the results. In such a case, the 80 per-cent are not unhappy, but you can count on the fact that the best performers are unhappy. It is not a good management strategy to punish your best performers.

Pay for performance works. Because money is a positive reinforcer to almost everyone, you will get more of what you compensate. The most important point to be determined in pay-for-performance plans is what constitutes valuable per-formance.

An increasing number of insurance companies are

compensating hospitals and doctors on pay-for-perform-ance plans. While some reports describe successful results, (Science Daily, 2008) numerous articles are claiming that this system doesn't work (Glickman, et. al. 2007). Hospitals are paid for the improvement of a variety of quality and patient safety measures, such as providing heart patients with aspirin immediately on admission and giving antibiotics to pneumonia patients within four hours. Doctors are paid for timely diagnosis and for the use of specific drugs for specified conditions.

The critics actually validate that the P4P, as it is often referred to, does work. The problems come from the wrong behavioral contingencies of reinforcement, not from this par-ticular method of pay. One critic says that it is pay for com-pliance, not pay for performance. Well, if compliance is increasing, then the pay system is working. The fact that the increased compliance does not necessarily benefit the patient is a problem of design. Another critic says the system encourages doctors and hospitals to "cherry pick" patients, meaning that they select only relatively healthy patients. This indicates that the plan is working. It tells us that doctors have changed their behavior to favor healthy patients at the exclu-sion of the very ill. This is not a fault of the method but, again, the contingencies of reinforcement in the plan.

Annual bonuses can be a problem because most people who receive bonuses don't know specifically what they per-sonally did to earn them. Bonuses are typically given at the end of the year and in spite of some statement by manage-ment that the bonus is for the employee's hard work, a strong and specific connection between the work of the individual and the bonus just doesn't exist. Even though the bonus is probably a positive reinforcer, without a way to track how the bonus is being earned on a week-to-week or month-to-month basis, the bonus is too delayed to have a strong impact on specific behaviors.

Profit sharing is a good way to give employees more money because the company can always afford to do it and is usually happy to do it. However, from a behavioral perspective it suffers from the same problems as performance pay and bonuses. When money is distributed on the basis of non-performance criteria and on group accomplishment, time and money are wasted.

Thomas Gilbert would say that the uses of money described above "devalue the instrument." Money is a powerful positive reinforcer and as such can generate fantastic financial results, morale, and teamwork, or it can literally destroy an organization. Let's turn now to some ways to make the use of money work for you rather than against you.

 ## WHAT TO DO INSTEAD

All of the problems with compensation described above, according to the science of behavior analysis, are basically problems of contingencies of reinforcement. Contingencies of reinforcement may be stated, implied, and/or actual contingencies of reinforcement. A stated contingency is, "You will receive a sales commission of 10 percent for every sale you make." An implied contingency may be that "if you work hard, you will get a raise." The actual contingency may be that you work hard and are assigned more work. An example that most parents are familiar with involves a prize in the bottom of a cereal box. The implied contingency is that when the cereal is eaten, the child can get the prize. The actual contingency is that the child can pour the cereal out and get the prize without eating the cereal or can get the prize by opening the box from the bottom. While one might say that the child is cheating if he does either, the problem is not so much with the child as with the contingency. The design should be such that the child can get the prize only after eating the cereal. When employees don't follow the rules and get the reinforcer, the fault lies in the design or in the management of the process.

One thing we know for certain is that you get more of what you reinforce. Because money is such a powerful reinforcer it can often reinforce problem behavior, even when the money was not meant to reinforce such behavior. If behavior or performance is not what you expected or wanted, rather than going back to a less effective form of pay, such as hourly or salary, simply change the contingencies of reinforcement.

EFFICIENT USE OF A BEAUTIFULLY-HONED INSTRUMENT

Changing the way people are paid almost always involves emotional behavior because a large number of employees believe that changes in compensation favor the organization, not them. This is because changes often are associated more with bad economic times and poor organizational performance than good ones. So even when the changes put more money in employee's pockets, you can expect some initial skepticism. Over time as people experience increased income from contingent pay, they want to move from salary to contingent pay.

Because salary is the most common form of pay, doing away with it, as inefficient as it is, will cause a lot of turmoil. Therefore, I would suggest starting with a combination of base salary and some form of performance pay. Dickinson (1993) found that a performance bonus of as little as 3 percent of salary was as effective as one of 100 percent. It seems that the important variable is that there is an opportunity to earn above salary. LaMere, et. al. (1996) found that truck drivers significantly improved their performance when they were paid only 3 percent of their total pay in incentives (in comparison to their previous hourly pay). Interestingly, going from 3 percent to 10 percent did not result in any further increases in performance. The data were collected for four years and the increases were sustained. Therefore, that study demonstrates that even though the incentives constitute a small proportion of a person's total pay, performance increases are long-lasting.

There are at least three things that must be done to get the best results. One is to pinpoint the behaviors and results that add value to the enterprise. This is time-consuming and difficult, but is the most important part of the process. If you don't have a clear description of the results and supporting behaviors, you are bound to get an inferior result.

Second, you must have an easy way to measure the results and behaviors. In the book, *Performance Management,* (Daniels and Daniels, 2004) my co-author and I describe in detail whether to focus on behavior or results. A very large number of managers believe that they supervise jobs that can't be measured. I don't believe that to be true. I agree that it is difficult and time-consuming, but I know it is worth the trouble and the time. I like Peter Drucker's method for determining job measures (Drucker, 1971). He said to stop doing the job and see what changes. Whatever changes is the measure. If nothing changes, eliminate the job! If the point of measurement is to help the performer earn more money, believe me, measures will be found.

Third, the measure should be one that can be easily tracked by the performer. The most effective form of performance feedback is immediate. If employees know at any point in time how they are doing, the receipt of pay can be delayed until the agreed-upon pay period. The important part of the design is that the performers are able to track their performance in relation to a potential payout. For example, let's say that an employee is eligible for .01 percent of annual profit depending on his performance. If the performer knows that his performance is 850 on a 1000 point scale, he knows that he would get 85 percent of the .01 of the profit allotted to him.

Abernathy (1996) has proposed Profit-Indexed Performance Pay as an efficient and effective form of compensation. It has been successfully implemented in a wide variety of organizations throughout the country. Abernathy is a behavior analyst and his system overcomes the problems of the conventional pay systems. In his system, all additional compensation to base salary is paid against the company's profit. Each performer has a performance matrix (similar to the one in Appendix A) and gets a scorecard each month showing the amount of performance pay earned that month, given that the company is profitable.

In structuring any pay system, make certain that you include all the aspects of the job as a requirement for the pay. For example, as described previously, if the top commissioned salesperson makes sales but treats the staff badly and is derelict in paperwork, only pay when the paperwork is completed in a timely manner to some pre-determined level of quality. Measures of the impact of his/her behavior on the staff and of teamwork with other salespersons should be included.

In piecework the same applies. The pay is determined not just by the number of quality pieces completed but may also include variables such as the condition of the work area at the end of the day and use of materials and equipment. When people take a job where the conditions of earning a commission or piece-rate are spelled out in precise terms, there is rarely any argument. Lincoln Electric has the oldest piecework pay system in the country, over 100 years old. The efficiency of this system has allowed the company to award bonuses every year often equal to their annual piece-rate compensation.

As Gilbert would say, money is a powerful reinforcer and as such, you get what you pay for. Use the behavior of the performers as a diagnostic test of what you are actually reinforcing vs. what you intended to reinforce. It does no good to blame the performer for continuing to engage in the behavior that you are reinforcing and rewarding. Make sure that the implied or stated contingencies match the actual contingencies on the job to truly capture the motivational power of money.

o   o   o   o   o   o

#7
"YOU DID A GOOD JOB, BUT . . . "

> The meanest, most contemptible kind of praise is
> that which first speaks well of a man and then
> qualifies it with a "But,"
>
> *–Henry Ward Beecher (1813-1887)*
>
> I know no manner of speaking so offensive as
> that of giving praise and closing it with an exception.
>
> *–Sir Richard Steele (1672-1729)*

Many adults remember when as children they brought home a school report card with five A's and one B only to have the parent say, "What about that B?" When I was in clinical practice, I witnessed the impact of well-meaning but devastating parental practices that were intended to cause children to do their best.

The father of one of my former patients always made negative comments for every accomplishment his daughter made, even into adulthood. No matter what she did he would always make a negative comment. Although she had many accomplishments to be proud of, she never had a feeling of satisfaction because she always had been made to feel that she should have done better. The unexpected result was that the more she accomplished, the more depressed she became. At the point she became too depressed to care for her children and herself, her husband brought her for treatment.

Although her analysis of her father's behavior was that he hated her, I saw it differently. I thought the reason he did what he did was because he cared a great deal for her. He thought that by pointing out her faults, he was helping her to always do her best. The problem was that even though his behavior was well-intentioned, it was one of those screwy common sense ideas that actually produced the opposite of what he intended.

THE BOSS' BUT

"You did a good job, but . . ." is the business version of this story. For many managers and supervisors saying, "You did a good job, but . . ." is almost a compulsion. Whether it is because the manager has too much to do in the time available, whether it is to let the performer know that there remains much to do, or whether it is thought to be a motivational device, it is an ineffective management practice. "You did a good job, but you know you still have a long way to go," is the classic. The effect of such a statement is to cause people to ignore the first part and obsess on the last part. It is not uncommon that the response to peers following this statement from a manager is, "No matter what you do around here, you can never please him." What is intended to be a positive consequence often turns out to be a punisher. Motivation is decreased, rather than increased. Therefore, time could be better spent.

Many managers believe that if you don't let people know you are not completely satisfied, they will stop improving. Also, I have heard many managers say that if you brag on people they will become self-satisfied and quit improving.

It is important to know that if performers quit after being praised, it indicates at least one of two problems. The first is that if the performer stopped improving, the praise was not a positive reinforcer. This is true because positive reinforcement increases behavior. The other possibility is that the improvement was generated by negative reinforcement, not positive reinforcement.

The way to tell which consequence causes the behavior is to see what happens following the attempted praise. If performance drops, then you know that the praise was not a reinforcer but a punisher because punishment decreases behavior. On the other hand, if the behavior remained at the same level, chances are that it was being driven by negative reinforcement.

There is little doubt that "yes, but" does not motivate and is more often a punisher. It becomes a prodding, nagging style of management that loses any effectiveness quickly and is clearly a waste of time and money.

 ## WHAT TO DO INSTEAD

To know what to do, you should ask yourself the question, "What am I trying to accomplish by this practice?" If the goal is to motivate the person or group to do more, it doesn't. Therefore, a different response is needed.

When you positively reinforce improvement, employees will seek information, coaching, and training that will help them improve. This is one of the indicators of a positively reinforcing culture—the voluntary effort to improve. When focusing on mistakes, people become defensive, and blame others, blame equipment, suppliers, and customers.

Many managers have a difficult time providing positive reinforcement for improvement, particularly small improvement. They have never had the experience of seeing people blow the goals away. Growing up in a stretch goal culture where difficult goals are the rule, the tendency is to set few large goals rather than many small goals.

The primary role of a manager is not to correct employee mistakes. While mistakes cannot be ignored, it turns out that the most effective way to get people to learn from their mistakes is to focus on improvement, not mistakes. Unquestionably, the fastest path to excellence is to create an improvement culture. You do that by valuing improvement. What that means is that the organization that recognizes and positively reinforces the smallest improvement will make the fastest change since positive reinforcement accelerates behavior.

In talking about this with managers, two questions arise:

1. **"What about performance appraisal?** Don't you have to deal with both the good and the bad in the appraisal meeting?" By now you understand what I think about performance appraisal. However, I understand that even though most people reading this agree that it is a waste of time and money, they do not have the option of eliminating it.

In the typical performance appraisal session where the good and the bad are given, it is almost never satisfactory to either party. This is because the average person at work sees suggestions for improvement during the appraisal process as criticism. If you have a negative reinforcement culture, you will find employees becoming defensive, argumentative, resistant to suggestions for change, and tending to blame others for their shortcomings.

On the other hand, if you have a culture that is characterized by frequent positive reinforcement for improvement, the employees will ask for negative feedback since the culture has demonstrated that improvement leads to increased positive reinforcement. In such cases, giving the positive and the negative at the same time is not a problem.

2. **"You can't just ignore mistakes, errors, poor quality, etc., can you?"** "Do you just give the positive without dealing with the negative?" The answer, of course is, "No." If your job is to help performers be successful, you need to give them the information and apply the consequences that will promote improvement. The issue is when to do it.

GOOD NEWS; BAD NEWS: WHICH DO YOU GIVE FIRST, AND WHEN?

Separate the good from the bad. By that I mean let some time pass between the two. This relates to the old question that you have probably heard many times, "I've got some good news and some bed news; which do you want first?" Always give the good first. "You had an 8 percent improvement in your process quality this week. I am really pleased with your progress." At a later time, it could be an hour or a day, talk again about what she needs to do to get to standard performance. "Betty, what do you think you can do to get to standard by the end of the month?" "Jim, I like your report. It is concise and you completed it ahead of schedule. Thank you." The next morning, "Jim, I was thinking about your report and if you will make these two changes, I believe the report will be even better."

Research by Brewer (1989) and Roberts (1997) on the effects of the timing of positive and negative feedback in corporate training situations have shown similar results. Their studies investigated the effects on performance when the good news and the bad news were given at the end of the training session versus giving the students the good news at the end of the session and waiting till the next session to talk about opportunities for improvement. These studies show that the latter is two to three times more effective than giving both the good and the bad at the same session. Figure 3, on the following page, is data from Robert's (1997) research on teaching students to translate English to Japanese. The line with the squares is the traditional method of giving feedback at the end of the session when the good and the bad news was given at the same time. The top line (circles) shows that when the good news was separated from the bad, learning was clearly more efficient.

Figure 3

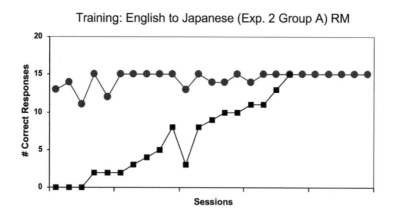

Training: English to Japanese (Exp. 2 Group A) RM

CULTIVATING AN IMPROVEMENT CULTURE

In summary, most performance problems are solved when you create a culture where improvement is valued. The smaller improvement you detect and reinforce the better. With frequent positive reinforcement people are more open to opportunities for improvement. When you focus on the positive behavior or accomplishments, it is not uncommon that the performers will point out where they could have done better, thereby eliminating the need for the manager to bring this to their attention.

When I talk of a positive reinforcement culture, I mean one where positive reinforcement is a daily and frequent occurrence. It is not something that you turn on and off; rather, it is the way you approach behavior in the workplace. You begin the day by assuming that the vast majority of employees come to work wanting to do their best for the company. If you are providing frequent positive reinforcement for improvement and providing individual and group feedback but still have performance problems, look first at the work environment to see if it has been designed to bring out the best in people. Check to see if work has been made difficult by policies, procedures, and work processes. If the workplace has been properly designed and you still have problems, check to see how the employee performed in training. *The last place you look for a cause of poor performance is at the employee.* Unfortunately, it is often the first place most managers and supervisors look.

Ron Dennis is one of my favorite managers. He really understands behavior. He is a distribution center manager in Zanesville, Ohio. In a center with about 700 employees he has terminated only two employees for performance issues over a three-year period, an incredible record to most people acquainted with the industry. The reason is that whenever there is a performance issue with an employee, the first question he asks of his managers is, "How did we fail that person?" The managers look at their records from recruitment, training, and prior performance on the floor. In all but two cases, they found that there was some management failure that prevented the performance they needed.

A positive performance culture is characterized by energy, excitement, and enthusiasm, as well as by people seeking information and feedback that will help them improve. If you don't have that culture and are trying to develop a positive management style, check your personal behavior in relation to the "yes, but."

o   o   o   o   o   o

#8
THE SANDWICH

I thought he was going to chew me out, but he bragged on me.

–A manufacturing employee

The sandwich method of correcting performance is probably the most common way that managers are taught to deal with poor performance. It is called the *sandwich method* because criticism is sandwiched between two positive statements. To some people this sounds a lot like *You did a good job, but . . .*, which is actually an attempt at positive reinforcement with the intent of causing the performer to continue improving an already good performance. The sandwich method corrects some behavior or performance with the intention of stopping undesirable behavior and increasing the more appropriate behavior.

Psychologists have recommended this technique of correcting behavior because it "protects the ego" of the performer and makes him more responsive to the criticism. Here is a typical psychological explanation of the process:

> *When delivering a critique, it's important to censure the behavior, not the individual. One of the easiest ways to encourage receptivity is to preface your criticism with a positive statement about the person's job performance or character. Once you've fortified his ego, deliver the bad news. Ensure that he received the message and knows how to correct the situation. Then close the conversation with an affirmation.*

I know of no research that supports this technique as being effective.

Consider this. "You are one of the best employees we've got, when you are here. If you don't improve your attendance in the next two months, we are going to have to terminate you. Why, you have more talent in your little finger than most people have in their whole body and that is why I am so concerned about you."

WHAT'S YOUR POINT?

What is the received message here? You may not hear until some time later that you are the best employee or how much talent you have, unless you happen to screw-up or continue to miss work. At best the impact of this type of interaction has been diluted by the two positive comments. Show me some objective data that this actually produces a behavior change quicker than a more straightforward approach. I don't believe such data exists. The person it helps the most is the one giving the bad news. Since most managers have trouble correcting employee performance, starting and ending with positives makes it easier to do. From what we know about how to change behavior, the sandwich method it is not an effective practice for at least two reasons.

First, since the ultimate purpose of this technique is to improve performance of some kind, reinforcement for the desirable behavior is necessary. Punishment stops behavior. Stopping inappropriate or ineffective behavior does not guarantee that the more effective or appropriate behavior will take its place. Since there are almost always more ways to do something wrong than to do something correctly, the probability is that when the wrong behavior is stopped, another wrong behavior will take its place.

Second, if you use sandwiching frequently you will create a *waiting for the other shoe to drop* syndrome. Employees get to the point where they don't want to hear they've done something well because they know that it is probably a prelude to criticism.

Janis Allen, a behavioral consultant, tells the story (Allen and Snyder, 1990) of a manager who did not have a habit of being positive but had been through our Performance Management (PM) training and was trying to do better. He went into an employee's office and said, "Lisa, I just saw the report you wrote and this letter is excellent. You have saved me considerable time here and I appreciate it. I didn't know you knew precisely what I wanted, but this is exactly how I would have done it. This is great!" She stared at him without making a comment. Soon the silence became unbearable and as he turned to run, she called out, "Alex, what did you *really* come out here for?" Lisa was waiting for the other shoe to drop because it was very unusual for Alex to talk to her for the sole purpose of thanking her for doing a good job. His straightforward and sincere compliment made her suspicious. How common is that?

Sadly, this scenario is so common that people tell me they wish they had known this technology 20 years ago. As they learn about behavior, the first thing that occurs to them is how this applies to their relationships at home. Of course, I have said the same thing. And though I'm a behavior analyst, I am also human, so I know how difficult it can be to follow my own advice.

Unfortunately, one of the habits I had in dealing with problematic behavior of my children was that the time I was most likely to tell my girls, "I love you" was after I had disciplined them. As they cried I found myself saying something like, "Now honey I hate to do this but the reason I do is because I love you and I am concerned about your future." Of course now I know that not only was my timing bad, but they were in no mood to hear what I said, much less believe it.

 ## WHAT TO DO INSTEAD

If you have some corrective feedback to give someone, give it in a straightforward manner. State it in terms of the problem behavior and state the specific, desired behavior to take its place. Then state the consequences. Ask for questions and end the meeting. "Tim, you have been late three days this week. I have spoken to you about this before and you know how important it is for you to be here on time because other employees cannot complete their work until you do yours. If you are late again this month, you will be terminated. Do you have any questions? Now, what can I do to help you be punctual?"

It is of course very important that you then observe the performance so you can see and respond to any improvement. Being on time should now trigger positive reinforcement, but improvement in any aspect of performance should occasion some positive interaction. Even increased social reinforcement for good performance at work increases the incentive to be on time.

It's often helpful to have the performer track the behavior you want on a graph. Of course you should review it frequently. In the case of tardiness mentioned above, don't focus on the tardiness because he could be on time every day and still not get parts to others on time or in the right condition. Rather, you track the number of quality assemblies delivered to colleagues on time. A benefit of this focus is that you address the tardiness problem as well as the productivity issue.

> A supervisor had a highly skilled performer who was missing about one or two days a month. According to the attendance policy he was on the verge of being fired. The supervisor called him in and discussed his record and the policy. The policy stated that if a given number of absences occurred during a quarter, the person would be terminated. After reviewing the policy with the performer, the supervisor pulled out a graph showing the date on which he would be fired if he continued to miss work at the current rate. The supervisor told the employee that he wanted to meet with him each week and they would plot the date of his firing as modified by his attendance the previous week. Of course, very quickly it became a positive meeting where they laughed and talked about how much he was improving. Not only did he make a dramatic change in his attendance but both his outlook and performance improved.

Once in a while, in every workplace, behavior needs to be corrected. However, when done effectively, there should be fewer and fewer times when this is necessary. If the number of occasions where correction is necessary does not decrease over time, you may be getting positive reinforcement for punishing! It is easy to fall into the punishment mode of management since people most often make some immediate visible reaction to punishment which is usually positively reinforcing to the one doing the punishing. Be careful that you don't fall into this trap. You will know you are in this trap if you find that an increasing amount of your time is spent correcting performance.

WHAT TO DO INSTEAD
(Four Ways to Avoid the Sandwich)

1. USE 4-TO-1 *(a four-to-one ratio)* AS A GUIDE TO YOUR VERBAL INTERACTIONS

Years ago when I first started working in industry, I was asked numerous times about the balance between positive reinforcement and punishment. In some data collected from supervisors and managers, we found that the average reported ratio was about 2:1. In other words, they attempted to positively reinforce twice as often as they attempted to correct. I suspect that an objectively observed ratio would have been considerably lower than the self-reported ratio.

In looking for research to suggest a data-based guideline, I found two studies that had investigated the issue. Madsen and Madsen (1974) conducted some research on the relationship of reinforcers and punishers in public school classrooms and found that when teachers had rates of positive reinforcement to punishment of 4:1 or better, their classrooms were characterized with high achievement and good classroom discipline. When the rates dropped below 4:1, achievement and behavior deteriorated. In a similar vein Stuart (1970) found that among parents of delinquents, positive reinforcement/punishment rates were about 1:1. When they looked at parents with no delinquent in the family, the positive reinforcement/punishment ratios approximated 4:1. A more recent study by Hart and Risley (1995) observed family interactions between parents and young children and found the positive reinforcement/punishment ratios in families with professional parents were in the range of 6:1; the families of working class parents had ratios of 2:1, and the families of welfare parents had ratios of 1:2.

Armed with the data from the first two studies, I set a target for managers and supervisors of an average of four positives to one negative over the course of a day, week, or month. Unfortunately, I found that some managers who had a negative interaction with an employee went looking for four things to positively reinforce. On the other hand, some felt that if they had delivered four positives, they earned the right to get on someone's case. Some thought it was an individual ratio and they would talk about owing individuals positives because they had given them negatives.

Even though a few misapplications and many jokes accompanied this ratio rule, the information sensitized the managers and supervisors to the positive behavior in the workplace and it always resulted in measurable performance improvement.

2. TRACK YOUR INTERACTIONS

I predict that you will discover you are not as positive as you think you are and that, if you track your behavior, you will begin to see the many things employees do every day that merit some approval. When correct behaviors increase, negative behaviors will automatically decrease. Remember that 4:1 is a guide not a goal. The ultimate goal is to increase the frequency of positive dialogue between you and employees. If you do this based on what I have detailed about positive reinforcement, you will be sure to receive the reward of better performance.

3. SEPARATE THE POSITIVES FROM THE NEGATIVE

If you find yourself in a situation where correcting behavior is necessary, do it without apology. Then, be alert to a time when a more productive behavior occurs and be sure to positively reinforce it. If you follow this advice, you will find fewer and fewer occasions occur where correction is necessary and many occasions where positive reinforcement is appropriate.

4. REMEMBER, SANDWICHING BENEFITS THE *SANDWICHER* MORE THAN THE *SANDWICHEE*

Keep your focus on the behavior that needs correcting. Don't dilute the impact of the interaction just because it is easier for you to talk about the positives. Save that for later when the person has shown some improvement in the target behavior.

In summary, poor performance should be dealt with in a direct manner. Over time, the occasions of correcting behavior should decrease and positive interactions should increase. No healthy workplace, or home for that matter, should contain more negative interactions than positive ones. One way to accomplish this is to adopt the perspective of Coach John Wooden, who said, "I rarely, if ever, criticized a player who tried in an intelligent way to make things happen on the court, even when he failed."

o   o   o   o   o   o

#9
OVERVALUING SMART, TALENTED PEOPLE

I worked hard. Anyone who works as hard as I did
can achieve the same results.

–Johannes Sebastian Bach

After the Enron (McLean et al., 2003) disaster you would think that anyone who understood what happened there would realize that an organization's success is not assured by having smart and talented employees. What Jeffery Skilling, while CEO of Enron, demonstrated was that smart people can learn bad behavior quickly. What Enron did, and others still do, was to waste a lot of time and money trying to find, hire, and retain smart, talented people. When Enron hired these outstanding people, they treated them special by routinely exempting them from following certain job requirements, policies, and procedures. Because they were labeled "smart" they got by with rude, insensitive behavior with other employees and in some cases with customers. Because of their behavior, bosses were constantly spending time cleaning up the messes that their special hires created with peers, subordinates, and other managers. Smart, talented people follow the same laws of behavior that everyone else does, so you do not need to (and shouldn't) treat them any more special than you do any other employee.

Why do we keep looking for smart people? Apparently the thinking is that smart, talented people are in short supply. The Web offers eight million ways to find advice about hiring and retaining talented employees. Without a doubt, every company should hire the best people available and I favor any means that promote this. However, smart, talented people are not in short supply; they are all around us.

UNDERVALUING EMPLOYEE POTENTIAL: THE COMMON PROBLEM

Contrary to popular opinion, you don't buy people's brains; you buy their behavior. If one person's brain helps him or her do something that another can't, that something should make the person more valuable, rather than their measured IQ. More importantly, employee value lies in how their intelligence is used to advance the mission and vision of an organization.

You can't tell if someone is smart by looking at a sheet of paper. Résumés can't tell you how well a person works with others or even how the person performed in all the jobs listed. Are the accomplishments listed on the candidates resume actually created by the applicant or accomplished in spite of him or her? In addition, just being smart doesn't mean that you have practical sense. We've all known people with high IQs who *don't have enough sense to come in out of the rain.*

In the beginning of my career as a clinical psychologist, I gave many intelligence tests. I regret most of them because parents, teachers, and others took the tests too seriously. *They thought the test measured what someone was capable of learning or doing.* No test can predict what a person is capable of learning or doing. An intelligence test may tell you what a child knows relative to those of the same age, but does not do very well at predicting future success.

Unfortunately many parents upon discovering that their child had a high IQ score would set unreasonably high goals for the child, resulting in failure, frustration, and withdrawal from normal academic pursuits. On the other hand upon finding the child had a low IQ score, many parents would scale back their expectations and would not expose them to things that might result in failure and frustration. Both decisions are wrong.

When I was the Head of Psychology Education and Training at Georgia Regional Hospital in Atlanta, Georgia, I required that the staff be prepared to teach three lessons that exceeded a special-needs child's current accomplishments. Teachers were measured by how much a child learned, not by whether the child was performing according to what was expected based on his or her IQ score. As a result we were surprised every day by what these children learned to do.

I have said numerous times that if you have every job filled, you have the smartest people you need. While I admit this statement is somewhat of an exaggeration, the intent is to make the point that if your organization is not designed to bring out the best in the people you have, what do you think such conditions will do to smart, talented people? The reason that companies think there is a shortage of smart talented people is that their systems, processes, and practices are designed to produce only a few of them. Skilled people are often in short supply, but people with the talent and brains to develop skills are most likely already in your employ. Anders Ericsson, a world renowned researcher on expertise, believes that you can teach virtually anyone to be an expert in almost anything.

Ericsson's (1991) research shows that the relationship between exceptional performance and IQ is very weak. He says, "For scientists, engineers, and medical doctors who complete the required education and training, the correlations between ability measures and occupational success are only around .02." In other words, there is no correlation. Your problem is not that you don't have enough smart people. You can hire the most brilliant performer in the world and if your management practices are poor, the person will leave your employ or will perform like all the rest of those with lesser ability.

The processes and procedures by which employees are appraised and rewarded tend to make it look like there are only a few smart people, when in fact there are many. Under the right circumstances, most people can develop into high performers. We now have efficient technology and training methods that allow us to get performers to high levels of skill in a fraction of the time usually required.

FLUENCY: PERFORMANCE THAT IS QUICK, EASY, AND ACCURATE

We revised a training program for an insurance company where classroom training was cut by over 34 percent; and on-the-job training was reduced from 26 weeks to three weeks! Trainees were performing at the level of seasoned and skilled performers by week three of training. The behavioral technique used to create these results is called *fluency*. *Fluency* is defined in this context as automatic, non-hesitant responding. Using fluency methods in a distribution center, they developed what they called "Accelerated Individual Training." Their old approach, using traditional methods of training, took from six to eight weeks to get employees to standard. Using fluency techniques, the time was reduced to six to seven days.

What Ericsson discovered is that anyone can become an expert in anything if he puts in 10,000 hours of deliberate practice. I think that is a profound discovery. Think about it. You can become an expert in something you've dreamed of even at your age. All you have to do is to find a way to put in the 10,000 hours of deliberate practice. By the way, playing 18 holes of golf does not count as four hours of deliberate practice. What counts is time reading about how to play the game, time spent with an instructor, and then time on the range trying to become fluent in what you have learned—*deliberate* practice.

The interesting thing about Ericsson's research is that the experts he studied were using traditional methods of training. I have a research interest in learning what would happen if the number of positive reinforcers in the training were doubled or tripled? Would it cut the number of hours in half or by two-thirds? I don't know the answer but we are planning research to find out. I suspect that increasing the frequency of positive reinforcement during the training will substantially cut the number of hours required for gaining fluency.

Morningside Academy (Snyder, 1992) has shown amazing

academic progress with learning disabled children and adults. Morningside offers a money-back guarantee if children do not gain two or more years of academic progress per academic year of study. With adults the guarantee is two years of progress per month! In over 25 years of existence, the academy has never returned tuition because the school's improvement rate is close to three years per one year of enrollment. To give you an idea of how the school does this, in third grade math a student may do over 1000 math facts a day! In the public schools a student will be lucky to do 50 per day. In the previous insurance example, we increased the number of problems the student had to solve in the training from approximately 50 to over 800.

I do not have the space here to devote to the fluency research, but at the risk of oversimplification, I will tell you that it relies on high rates of responding, or what educators used to call *drill* or *rote memory*. While these techniques meet with general disfavor in schools, the research consistently shows that people learn significantly faster and retain significantly more when trained under this type of curriculum as opposed to the current approach.

In today's economy with fast growth and rapid technological change, the ability to develop people quickly to high levels of skill in short time frames is very desirable. A client in India has the challenge of hiring 6000 employees in six months and making 1000 of them managers in that same period of time. Such a challenge cannot be met with traditional training methods and techniques. Nor can it be met with distance learning and traditional computer-based training. Managers who aren't acquainted with fluency techniques will find themselves at an increasing competitive disadvantage when their competitors adopt fluency methods of training.

WHAT TO DO INSTEAD

1. Be aggressive in training and promoting people.

A young aircraft engineer approached me after my speech and wanted to give me an example of how his company didn't understand positive reinforcement. He said there was a job that he wanted to learn as he thought it would help him in the future, so he approached his manager about it. The manager said he needed him where he was and actually gave the young engineer a raise to show how valuable he was. The mistake his boss made, he felt, was that he wanted the experience of the other activity and was already happy with the money he was making. Shortly after this incident, a competitor offered him a job that allowed the opportunities he requested from his present employer. He said, "My former boss actually did me a favor, I guess, because my new employer is going to match my current salary and I now have the opportunity to learn the new skills I wanted."

As a manager it is your job to retain and develop people. Employee retention is not a human resource responsibility. A part of any reward system for managers and supervisors should be the number of employees they keep and promote within the organization. One of the most innovative programs of this nature occurred at Kodak a number of years ago. When black-and-white photographic paper manufacturing was considered to be a dying part of the business by many new hires, it became increasingly difficult to recruit them to this part of the business when there were jobs available in other parts of the company. Joe Stoudenmeyer, the department manager, turned that situation around in a single year by rewarding supervisors and managers for promoting their best people out of the department. Managers would actually *sell* other departments on their employees because the managers were rewarded for getting their best employees better and higher paying jobs. If a job didn't exist in the company, the managers would explore possibilities outside of the company. Although that didn't occur frequently, it was an option. Joe thought it was important for the company to make sure that their employees knew that the department management had their best interests at heart. Of course, many didn't want to leave because Paper Sensitizing became such a positively reinforcing place to work.

2. **Spend the time and money to train people to fluency.** Whether it is in sales or operations, one of the most costly mistakes companies make is to put people in jobs before they are fluent in the critical aspects of the job. The place this is most obvious to the average consumer is in what Clark Howard, a popular consumer advocate, calls "customer no-service." People dealing with the customer should be the most knowledgeable about products and services and know it so well that they can respond to customer problems correctly and without hesitation. To get people to this point requires training beyond the point of passing a quiz or demonstrating knowledge only one time. The amount of repetition required for fluency is far more than the average

trainer understands, but the extra time pays off in happier customers and more confident and competent employees.

3. **Have a way of positively reinforcing and rewarding employees who put in extra time and effort.** This requires observing behavior to make sure that those people who put in the extra effort are not overlooked or ignored. The benefit of getting managers to actually observe performers pays huge dividends in discretionary effort. Robert Eisenberger (1992) demonstrated in his research that people who are rewarded for extra effort not only work harder on assigned tasks but also work harder on other tasks as well. In addition they tend to be more honest and exert a higher degree of self-control. He says it this way:

> An increased secondary reward value of high effort, resulting from a developmental history of rewarded high performance in varied settings, might reduce the tendency to take advantage of dishonest shortcuts in pursuit of difficult goals. And, some individuals generally work harder than others. My *learned industriousness theory* states that if an individual is rewarded for putting a large amount of cognitive or physical effort into an activity, the sensation of high effort takes on secondary reward properties that lessen effort's general aversiveness. In accord with this view, research indicates that reward for high effort involving one or more activities increases the subsequent effort exerted in other activities.

The knowledge and technology exists today to create a high performing workplace with the people you have now. Money and time are better spent on growing smart, talented people rather than trying to entice and buy them.

TWO THINGS TO REMEMBER

1. You can teach anyone to do anything if you are smart enough.

2. You don't teach someone to the limit of their ability; you teach them to the limit of your ability.

o o o o o o

#10
THE BUDGET PROCESS

If you want a kitten, start by asking for a horse.

–Naomi, 11 years old

Naomi has learned the first rule of the budget game early in life. That rule is *ask for more than you need in the hope that you will get just what you need.* Managers learn the budget game quickly or they don't survive. Of course, your boss played this game when he was in your position and is currently playing it with his boss. Everyone is playing and everyone knows it.

I learned the game in my first year as head of the Department of Psychology Education and Training at Atlanta's Georgia Regional Hospital. In a state psychiatric hospital, you never have enough staff to do all the treatment needed so I started training volunteers to assist the units with patient treatment where appropriate. Volunteers earned the right to attend special training in applying behavioral solutions to their individual and family problems. The program was so successful that we had over 1000 active volunteers for a patient population of 500 and I did not have to fill all the staff positions. Because of an outstanding Volunteer Services Director and her work to get goods donated, the department had a year-end surplus of over $200,000. I was pleased with this result until I learned that my budget for the next year was cut by an amount equal to the surplus. It was the last surplus I ever had.

A similar experience occurred about the same time while I was a Vocational Rehabilitation consultant doing intelligence and vocational testing. Jim, a counselor in the department, was one of the most conscientious persons about spending money on clients I have ever known. He would look in the Sunday paper for specials on anything that he needed to purchase for his clients such as glasses, hearing aids, and medical supplies. He called therapists to find the best price for treatment. If his clients were not making progress in therapy, he stopped it. Because of his excellent money management, he had about 80 percent of his budgeted funds remaining with a little over three months remaining in the budgeted year. Believe it or not, the department director took money from his budget and gave it to another counselor who had spent his entire budget and needed more to serve his clients for the next quarter.

These experiences taught me that I should always spend all the money in the budget. Although I thought of myself as a responsible and hardworking employee, I spent any funds remaining toward the end of the fiscal year on equipment and supplies that I anticipated needing for future programs. Unfortunately some of those anticipated programs never became reality and the equipment probably remains in the warehouse 40 years later. How wasteful is this?

ENCLOSED IS A HAT—IF YOU CAN FIND IT

Because all bosses know you are playing the game, they never accept your budget as submitted. It is usually difficult for the boss to know where the *real fat* is because managers become expert at hiding money. My brother tells a story of a technician, Jim Clark, who assisted him on a sale when he was working with Union Carbide in their welding products division. In the course of demonstrating the product, the customer burned a hole in Jim's hat. Jim included the price of a new hat on his next expense report. Finance turned it down with a terse note, "We do not pay for hats." When he submitted his next expense report, Jim included a note, "Included is one hat if you can find it." Because the boss can't find the hats in most budgets, they are always sent back for rework so as to squeeze the hidden hats out of the amount requested.

These days most bosses ask for a bare-bones budget, but most managers learn that it is folly to prepare one. A young manager in an electric utilities company told me that when his boss asked for bare-bones, he prepared one. When his peers found out what he had done, they laughed at him. He reminded them that the boss said that if they conscientiously prepared a bare-bones budget, he would not ask for further cuts. Of course, later in the year the boss did ask for further cuts. After the cuts, his peers now had about what they needed because they had padded their bare-bones budgets while the young manager was left to finish the year with much less than he really needed. Anyone in charge of a budget knows that it is foolhardy not to pad your request. If you pad your budget, there's an outside possibility that you will get what you ask for; and, if your initial request is cut, which is very likely, you will increase the chance that you will have what you really need.

One of the problems with this kind of budget development process is that it diffuses accountability. Of course if accountability is diffused, there is no accountability; when problems arise, everybody blames everybody else. A vice-president of a software development company had been hired to replace another because the company was hopelessly behind on deliverables and the product that was delivered was riddled with functional errors. The president said, "I want you to tell me how much money it will take to fix this problem." The new VP did his due diligence and announced, "It will take $10 million." The president responded, "You've got it." In doing so, the president fixed accountability. If he had said, "I will give you eight," or even, "Can you do it for $8 million?" true accountability would have been lost. If the new VP didn't deliver with the $8 million budget, he would always be able to say, "I told you I needed $10 million."

REDUCING EXPENSES:
WHO ARE THE BENEFICIARIES?

Budget development is only one part of the game, however. In many organizations salary and other bonus opportunities are tied directly or indirectly to the number of employees you manage or to the dollar amount of your budget. Do you see potential waste of time and money here? Managers who have large budgets to administer and a large number of employees to manage receive the higher salaries and benefits. These behavioral contingencies favor increasing budgets rather than reducing them.

John Davis, a behavioral psychologist and consultant, was trained as a Chinese interpreter by the Army. When he was stationed on an island in the South Pacific in the 1980s, he soon discovered that there was really no need for an interpreter in that particular Army installation. After he completed his tour and was about to rotate home, the Army as a part of an audit of the installation, wanted to question him about his soon-to-be-empty position. He told the auditors that there was no need for an interpreter and if someone told them otherwise to please come back and let him respond. To his amazement, the auditors concluded that there was a need for *two* interpreters. Now, one could say that John did not have all the necessary data to understand such planning by a higher level of the Army; but we will never really know, since the auditors never got back to John for further input. However, most people, knowing how the government works, would suspect that John was correct.

I am sure that if there was any incentive for commanders to reduce head count while still accomplishing their mission, the new position would have never been added and the old one would have been eliminated. What is the incentive for reducing the size of government or any other organization, after all? Are there any incentives for managers to reduce expenses? How about the front-line employees? What incentive do they have to do more with less? If becoming more efficient doesn't favor managers and the front-line employees of the organization, substantial reductions will rarely be made.

The late Art Buchwald, American humorist and longtime columnist for *The Washington Post,* proposed a plan to reduce the size of the Federal budget and as absurd as it seems on its face, I believe his proposal had real merit. He proposed that anyone in the government who could find a way to eliminate his/her job should be retired at full pay. Since he said that salary is a small part of keeping someone on the payroll because fringe benefits, space requirements, administration, and supervision comprise the majority of the cost, it would be a good deal for the taxpayers. Furthermore he said that if a department head could figure a way to eliminate his/her department he/she should not only be retired at full pay but in addition should receive a one-time bonus of 10 percent of the departmental budget!

I am convinced that this plan would work. Taxpayers might not like the idea of retiring government employees many years before retirement age, but they would definitely like what it would do to the size of the federal budget. I am confident the savings would be many billions of dollars.

The point is that budgets are not the problem; rather, the problem is the way they are managed. In the federal government and in private enterprise there is almost no personal incentive for employees to reduce costs. Most have to be coerced to do so. The reason that initiatives like Six Sigma and Lean Manufacturing are not more widespread is that employees often find that the long-term result of saving on expenses does not favor them.

If people are playing the budget game, it is obvious that the behavioral consequences favor playing the game. How can we stop the game playing and get people to work to produce the most efficient, effective organization?

WHAT TO DO INSTEAD

Some writers question whether we even need budgets. A number of writers feel that budgets should be eliminated; well, not eliminated but changed in order of operational priority. Hope (2003) says that executives spend approximately 25 percent of their time on budgeting and budget-related activities. While I would certainly not advocate eliminating budgeting, I believe that the process could be made significantly more effective.

Most financial officers would say that budgets are needed to plan for the results you want and to ensure that the resources are allocated in alignment with the strategic objectives. However, in actuality, the way budgets are used is to ensure that managers engage in certain behaviors and don't engage in others. It ensures that planning occurs, that resources are used wisely, that you have fiscal accountability, and that there are consequences for spending more than you planned to spend. The problem is that when these behaviors don't occur, organizations usually change the process and often add punishers for the ineffective behavior. Levels of approval are added; budget review meetings are increased; managers who don't meet their budgets are fired, demoted, drawn and quartered. Company executives almost never examine the process to discover where the reinforcers are for the wrong behavior or where the punishers occur for the correct behavior.

As it stands in most organizations, the budget process is tedious, time-consuming, and confrontational. Typically managers do not look forward to doing budgets. This is somewhat unnatural since the process is related to the future growth and development of the enterprise. Why would that not be exciting rather than tedious? The answer lies in the fact that there is little planning of positive consequences for creating an efficient and effective budget and managing it successfully.

In order to make productive changes in the process the usual question must first be asked, "What are we trying to accomplish?" The usual answer is to create an organization that uses its resources in the most effective and efficient manner. The next question should be, "How can we get people to be highly motivated to do this?"

I have several suggestions.

1. Lavishly reward those who get all of the people in their unit involved and excited about doing more with less. Of course this requires a plan in which all employees are positively reinforced when they do more with less. This means that the reinforcers meet the requirements enumerated on pages 10 and 11. It requires also that the manager cannot be rewarded when the improvement and savings are accomplished by negative management behaviors.

2. Managers who demonstrate the ability to do more with less should get more with which to manage. As mentioned earlier, it is a frequent practice for managers who spend all their money to actually get more. Wait a minute—spend more, get more; spend less, get less. Something is wrong with this picture. Many times the *more* comes from budgets where managers have been thrifty and conscientious with their budgets. Why not reverse the process? Those who do more with less get more the next time and those who overspent their budgets get less next time.

3. Change the relationship between size of the budget and the number of employees as the criterion for amount of compensation and bonuses. Reward managers for the behaviors they use to create results, not just on results alone. It really does matter how results are achieved. Enron, WorldCom, and HealthSouth are only three of hundreds of companies where executives' behavior has ended in jail time. As a matter of fact when you search the Web on "Executives in jail," you get over two million entries. Think of an organization where the highest paid people were not those with the biggest budget and the most employees but the ones who produced the most with the least resources.

4. Budget from the bottom up. Budgets are often done upside down. When the people at the top of the organization determine the results necessary for success in the budget period, that information should be sent to the front lines of the organization. Supervisors need to meet with frontline employees so that they can formulate a budget for what it will take to reach those targets. Once the frontline employees and the supervisors determine the behaviors and the budget necessary to accomplish the organization's targets, the first level manager should ask the question, "What do I need (money and resources) to support the front line? The department manager asks, "What do I need to support the shift managers?" The focus of the budget should be on helping the employees on the front line of the organization have what is necessary to meet and exceed the expectations of the customer.

5) Use non-tangible as well as monetary rewards for good budget performance. Joe Stoudenmeyer was probably the first department manager in the history of Kodak to have his budget approved as submitted the very first time. All others had to be reworked at least once, if not many times. His boss, Ron Heidke, rewarded him with this immediate budget approval because of his consistent high performance against his budgets in the past.

What do you think might happen if those who performed well against their budgets were rewarded by allowing them to include something that they have wanted to do in the past but were not able to do because of cost? It could be a pet project, an experiment managers want to conduct, or some new piece of equipment that had not been previously approved. None of this needs to cost a lot of money; almost anything added to the budget (that was unexpected and unrequested) will have a powerful impact on people involved in this process.

In the fast-paced business environment that we live in today (and it will only get faster), it becomes increasingly difficult to project financial needs even on a 12-month cycle. Therefore the budget process as we know it today must change significantly. This change requires streamlining the process by making it less burdensome, less time-consuming, and more fun for everyone in the organization. I believe these suggestions will do just that. The net result of these changes will be that the company becomes more competitive, profitable, and financially viable.

o   o   o   o   o   o

#11
PROMOTING PEOPLE NO ONE LIKES

If you are a failure at relationships,
you are likely a failure at everything

–Ben Stein

A number of years ago, I spoke at an Organizational Effectiveness conference in which I made the statement that managers are paid to be well-liked. An executive came up to me afterward and said, "I'm going to have to think about that." I know many others would feel the same. However, to me, the fact that an executive would even question the statement is a sad comment on the state of affairs in business today. The fact that people don't believe that managers who are well-liked can be more effective in producing results than those who are loathed is rather amazing in and of itself. The overwhelming number of managers who failed in my 40 years in business were not well-liked. Most were hard-nosed and some were downright mean. The story is told of an Army Captain who fashioned himself as a really tough commander saying to one of his sergeants, "Sergeant, I bet you hate me so much that when I die you will probably come spit on my grave." The sergeant replied, "No sir, Captain. I promised myself that when I get out of this man's Army, I'm not going to stand in line to do nothing."

Interestingly, though, tell-it-like-it-is managers often have a Dr. Jekyll and Mr. Hyde-like personality. They are well-mannered to their friends (and bosses) and rude, demanding, and unappreciative to their direct reports. I know a division president of a large company who was the epitome of a Southern gentleman. In social situations he was witty, inter-esting, easy to talk to, and interested in others. However, at work everyone was afraid of him and avoided him whenever possible because almost all employees who had interactions with him had been terrorized by him at some point.

The question that has to be asked is, "Why would he be like that?" The simple answer is that he had a long history of being reinforced for his negative behaviors at work. He con-fided to me that he knew he needed to change but knew it was improbable in that no one would call him on his verbally abu-sive behavior. This was insightful because as long as he yelled and screamed and got what he wanted with no negative con-sequences, his behavior would continue even when he knew that it was a bad practice. On the other hand, if he engaged in the same behaviors in social situations, he would have no friends because people who don't work for him don't have to put up with such behavior.

In addition to the reinforcement he got from direct reports, he was heavily reinforced by his bosses because he got results. One of the problems, as I see it, is that executives very often look only at results without looking at the behaviors used to get them. They look for people who are smart, hardworking, ambitious, and technically competent. Who wouldn't want this kind of person for a management/ leadership position? But what they often don't see is that the person is also arrogant, vindictive, selfish, and emotional. Thankfully, most of these people fail as leaders. The problem is that, in the meantime, they wreak havoc on the organization. Oh, they get results alright, but at what price?

CONSIDER THE COST

When costs associated with turnover, grievances, absenteeism, training, recruitment, and performance just high enough to meet the demands of a demanding boss are factored in, organizations eventually come to the conclusion that they can't afford such managers. The problem is that these costs are rarely computed and seldom, if ever, expensed against the manager's results.

In talking with a plant manager about one of his department managers who had an atrocious management style, he said, "But he is one of the most knowledgeable weaving managers in the business." I asked how much he was willing to pay for such a manager. When the cost of recruiting and training highly technical supervisors and weavers and the lost production from the transition was figured, those costs alone were over $500,000 a year. Adjusted for inflation it would be well over $2,000,000 today.

Over the years, I have seen some outrageous behavior that has been overlooked because the boss thought the supervisors and managers were very smart and/or because they were the most experienced at what they did and as such considered to be indispensable. The outrageous behavior included throwing temper tantrums, embarrassing staff at meetings, and yelling and screaming at individuals and groups. In one case a manager locked two of his supervisors in an unair-conditioned room with the lights out!

I can tell you that yelling, screaming, cursing, and public criticism have no place in today's workplace and such behavior is a significant waste of time and money. Any manager or supervisor who yells, screams, curses, and criticizes in public is a poor manager and should be fired! By the way, yelling, screaming, and cursing are almost always public. Employees hear about it quickly even if they are not present. These behaviors do not improve performance and over the long run are devastating to morale and leadership. In addition, they are directly opposed to almost every organization's stated values.

You've seen it many times. A coach pulls a player out of the game and *gets in his face.* Fans expect it. Tony Dungy, coach of the Super Bowl winning Indianapolis Colts football team, said in a recent interview that when he was hired the owners were not concerned that he was to be one of the first African-American head coaches, but were worried that his positive coaching style might not be effective.

Fans want coaches who are tough on players. Somehow they feel that such behavior indicates the coach's passion for winning and his ability to take quick corrective action. Behavioral research tells us that this is not an effective way to teach or improve performance of athletes or employees. Coaches get by with it for two reasons: 1) because of the high rate of reinforcers from the game, the fans, the other players, and the media, the players will put up with less than effective coaching and, 2) since in-your-face coaching is almost a universal style, it is difficult for players to escape it. Yet, this kind of coaching behavior never gets the most out of athletes. If Bobby Knight, the controversial basketball coach who engaged in outrageous negative behavior toward his players and referees, had the knowledge of behavior that Coach John Wooden of UCLA has, he may even have surpassed Wooden's winning record. Knight has great knowledge of the game but almost zero knowledge of what causes people to do their best. Many managers admire coaches like Knight because his management style is visible and action-oriented. However, his management behavior was an obstacle that limited his success. This style of management is even less effective at work because of the low rate of positive reinforcement at work compared to that of sports.

Yelling and screaming and public criticism are often associated with what are referred to as *tough managers.* It is a myth that tough managers are needed to bring out the best in employees. They never do. What keeps the myth alive is that negative reinforcement and punishment will improve performance in a poor performing organization. By being tough on poor performers (firing them), these managers send a message to the organization that you better do your job or else! This will typically lead to improved performance, at least temporarily. However, a negative reinforcement and punishment strategy only creates an organization that performs to stay out of trouble. The German president of an American-owned company said in his heavy German accent and with a certain amount of pride that the best positive reinforcer he could give was to tell an employee, "You have not displeased me." Knowing that you have not displeased the boss can hardly be said to be inspiring. An organization that performs to stay out of trouble will never excel.

YOU KNOW YOU MAKE ME WANNA SHOUT

While I understand how some actions of employees make you want to yell, scream, and even shake some people to get their attention, it is not acceptable in today's workplace nor is it effective. David Thompson in his book *Managing People* (1978) says, "Indeed from a profit point of view, what people say to each other and how they say it probably has more influence than any other kind of interaction in private industry. Verbal interactions can make or break a company."

So why do we think we need tough managers? There is a widespread belief that tough equals profit. All you need to do to witness this belief firsthand is to look at the major business magazines and read the descriptions of the executives on their front covers. The media often asks the question, "Is he/she tough enough to get the job done?" The data is obscured by the fact that in a negative reinforcement business culture, the toughest boss wins. A tough manager is usually described as someone who engages in straight talk, makes decisions quickly, holds people accountable, and terminates them quickly when they don't deliver. He typically trades on fear, although he sees himself as caring and approachable. Such managers do get performance change. So, if they do all that, what is the problem?

Negative reinforcement works to increase behavior and it often works to get incremental improvement year after year. Indeed most continuous improvement initiatives are driven by negative reinforcement. Employees will do whatever they have to do to avoid the punishment from this type of manager. The problem is that these managers never get the most out of people. They do get more from an organization than a manager who yells and screams and doesn't follow through (hold people accountable and deliver the consequences they said they would). But in terms of the success the organization could attain, they never get it. When comparing tough managers, the toughest wins. When comparing a tough manager with one who knows and follows the laws of behavior, the latter wins every time. Eventually tough managers reach a plateau in performance because there is a limit to how much abuse people will take.

I knew a hotel manager who couldn't have been more negative if he had worn a pistol and shot people when they didn't do what he wanted. When I approached the V.P. of Operations about him, he said, "You don't understand; he has the best back-of-the-house-cost in the company." However, when the other nine properties implemented a system of positive performance management, within six months that same manager had the poorest back-of-the-house-cost in the company. His numbers hadn't deteriorated; the others had improved so much, he was left behind. In his book, *It's Your Ship: Management Techniques from the Best Damn Ship in the Navy* (2002), Captain Michael Abrashoff illustrates time and again how positive management practices developed a crew that outperformed all the ships in the Navy.

WOULD YOU RATHER BE A WOODEN OR A KNIGHT?

These negative behaviors of managers are very difficult to change because there is so much reinforcement for them by the response of employees who are on the receiving end of the behavior. When someone yells and the recipient of the abuse jumps, the jumping provides positive reinforcement for the yelling. In addition, because the intent of such a manager is to create a high-performing organization, the behaviors seem right and necessary. They will tell you that they don't even like to do these things but that poor performers force them to do so.

John Wooden (2005), arguably the most successful college basketball coach in history, said, "In my 40 years of coaching, you will not find a player that can honestly tell you that he ever heard me use profanity." He said also, "Self-control in little things leads to control of bigger things." He prohibited profanity in practice and in games because as he said, "I felt that a player who couldn't control his language when he got upset during a scrimmage would be more likely to lose control in more damaging ways during the heat of a competition . . ." This is also the case in business. Managers who cannot control their emotions, (that is, their tongues), rarely elicit discretionary behavior from employees and always utilize more human capital to do the job than those who use behaviorally sound management behavior. Again to quote Wooden,

> But for me, the fear and ill feelings that arise from intimidation, punishment, and cruel words have far less power than pride. It is very hard to influence someone in a positive manner over the long haul when you antagonize and alienate that individual. In addition, once you've angered someone and created a feeling of animosity, then you're forced to waste additional time backing up and trying to smooth things over.

WHAT TO DO INSTEAD

I know of a large University where the Trustees finally hired a new president after several years of searching for the perfect candidate. Within six months everyone, including the Trustees, knew they had made a hiring mistake. Nevertheless, three years later they have still not corrected the mistake. I don't blame them because if they can't get it right after several years of looking, how many years will they need the next time to get it right? What should you look for in those you would promote? Here are some of the things to look at before you consider business skills and business knowledge.

1. **Are they well-liked?** Promote people who are well-liked. You can be well-liked and be an ineffective manager; you cannot be the most effective manager and not be well-liked. It is not about a popularity contest. I am not talking about doing things to get people to like you but about creating an environment where people feel that they are valued and appreciated every day because of the way they perform. The first cut in selecting people for any management or supervisory position should be whether they have a positive impact on people. Likeability is by no means the only trait that you look at, but it should be a show stopper if it is not present.

   Effective leaders create willing followers. Any manager who is not liked cannot create willing followers. Followers yes, but *willing* followers, no. When you know that over half of all people put in leadership positions fail (Hogan et al. (1994)), it must tell you that we are looking at the wrong things when selecting people for leadership roles. Unfortunately, what most look at is how smart the person is or what kind of results they have been associated with in the past. I say "associated with" because in many cases these results were created not because of the manager but in spite of him. I am sure that those charged with making the decision on the University president mentioned did not have much data on his behavior with his previous staff and did not have an adequate sample of his impact on the behavior of those who reported to him.

While there is very little about management and leadership that cannot be learned, people skills are the most difficult to teach. Even at that, there are a very large number of people who want to learn these important skills. Unfortunately, they often learn most by following poor leadership models. A friend, the president of a large newspaper, said that a senior editor at the paper resigned unexpectedly. This created a ripple effect of promotions in the organization. As he was waiting by the elevator toward the end of the day when the announcement of promotions was made, he overheard a man in a nearby office exclaim to a colleague, "And all this time I've been kissing the wrong ###!"

2. **Do they know the science of human behavior— Applied Behavior Analysis?** When managers learn basics of behavior, they can change their own behavior as well as the behavior of those they lead. Years ago a manufacturing plant manager asked me to talk to one of his supervisors to help determine if he was management material. He told me that the supervisor was trying hard but was only a marginal performer. I told him that I couldn't tell much by talking to him but suggested that we put him in training and see how he responded to coaching. The last time I heard about that supervisor, he was

a plant manager. As it turned out, he was a natural-ly positive person but was being positive at the wrong time. In some cases, he was positive when he should have been negative and other times he was positive when he should have ignored certain employee behavior. Because of his misguided actions, employees took advantage of his good nature. At that point, he became negative but could not pull that off either. When he learned about the proper use of behavioral consequences, he blossomed.

3. **Do they have a history of getting results with positive methods?** Since the best indicator of what people will do in the future is what they have done in the past, when someone is being considered for promotion, spend some time observing how he/she gets results. Results are a given, since a history of getting results typically flags people for promotion consideration, but their behavior is the real differentiator. Observe their conduct in meetings, in the workplace, and in social situations. Does the person make spending time in the work area a priority or does he/she spend most of the day in the office? Do employees approach the person or ignore him? Do employees smile, laugh, and generally look comfortable around the person? In meetings, do employees interact with the person easily, showing no fear of offering dissenting opinions or ideas?

4. **Can they describe to you the process they would use to improve the performance of an individual and a group?** Students in the Performance Management track at Florida State University develop a portfolio

of their work much like artists do. The student is able to show a prospective employer the kind of results they have achieved in the past and precisely how they got them. Behavior analysis teaches people how to tackle all performance issues using a precise technology that can easily be described to anyone. If a candidate for a management job cannot give you a detailed description of actions they would take to tackle typical business issues, you should have little confidence that they will represent you well in today's fast paced business environment.

When you know behavior from a scientific perspective, you will be able to design systems, policies, and procedures that bring out the best in people every day. You will be liked and people will have fun helping you create a healthy, profitable business.

o   o   o   o   o   o

#12
DOWNSIZING

It is only when the tide is out
that you can see who is swimming naked.

–Peter Drucker

In 2006 a blogger wrote, "So by 2010, I reckon that the CEO of Telstra will be the sole employee left in Australia and by 2015 he will finish the downsizing by firing himself."

Let me say at the outset that as a business person, I understand the appeal of downsizing. As sales slow and cash flow is depleted, the facts on the side of such action seem compelling. The problem is that, of the many reasons organizations downsize, it doesn't reliably accomplish any of them. Numerous studies show that downsizing doesn't increase performance; it doesn't increase profits; it doesn't decrease expenses; and, it doesn't even lead to staff reduction in the long term. Why do they do it? I can think of three primary reasons for downsizing:

1. Technology makes it a necessity. Computerization and technological innovation has often led to significant increases in performance with significantly fewer people. In a statement attributed to author Warren Bennis (2003), he said, "The factory of the future will have only two employees, a man and a dog. The man will be there to feed the dog and the dog will be there to keep the man from touching the equipment." Though an obvious exaggeration, some futurists think we are moving in that direction.

2. Wall Street likes it. The increase in stock prices following the announcement of a downsizing is so predictable that former Secretary of Labor, Robert Reich, introduced *the 7 percent rule* because the average increase in share price on the announcement of a downsizing is around 7 percent.

3. It produces an immediate increase in profits and cash flow. As such it is almost like heroin to an addict (a positive, immediate, certain (PIC) consequence for the downsizers). When times get tough, downsizing gives the company a quick hit; although, a 1994 Watson Wyatt Worldwide study (Gandolfi, 2005) of 148 Canadian companies found that 60 percent that downsized did not increase profitability and 40 percent had no reduction in expenses. There was also a similar finding in a study of 1005 organizations which downsized in the 1980s (Huber and Glick, 1995). Of those companies, 68 percent did not increase profits and 54 percent did not reduce expenses.

DOWNSIZING PEOPLE AND UPSIZING PROBLEMS

While many reports show that economic results of downsizing are mixed, the effects on the employees are not. The ones who are terminated obviously have feelings of insecurity and depression frequently accompanied by anger at management. The ones who remain have many of the same feelings. They wonder if they are next. They have feelings that the company doesn't care for its employees and often develop a profound distrust of management. One thing we know for sure is that, after a downsizing, the same amount of work now has to be done by fewer people. A cost that is rarely figured is the physical toll downsizing has on the remaining workforce. A study in Finland (Vahtera, et.al., 2004) found that when work increased due to fewer people, sick leave, and cardiovascular deaths increased significantly.

Apart from fear, what would be the motivation to take on the additional work? As I have said many times, fear as a motivator never brings out the best in employees. The act of downsizing never increases loyalty to the company and its management. As a result, when employees complain of being overworked and burned out, managers begin to rehire former employees as contract employees or contract the work out to other companies.

It is certain that downsizing is a waste of time because many weeks and even months are consumed by many people making the administrative decisions involved in the implementation of an action that produces questionable results. The waste of time and the resulting impact on performance is rarely calculated as a cost of downsizing.

I was attending a senior management meeting where the managers were talking about how they were going to cut expenses because of a serious slow-down in the economy. At the beginning of the year, management had announced that they needed a 5 percent reduction in manufacturing expenses in each of the next three years. At the end of the first quarter, they changed and said that they needed 5 percent in the present year but needed 10 percent in the following year. At the end of the next quarter they changed again saying that they needed 15 percent reduction in the next 12 months. At this meeting they were talking about what physical assets they might dispose of to help meet their 15 percent targets.

When I got up to speak, I asked how many employees were represented by the executives in the room. They replied, "Twenty-one thousand." I then asked if they knew how the employees referred to their various cost-cutting plans. They replied that they didn't know. I told them that the employees called the first cost-cutting plan the "triple nickel." The next one was the "nickel-dime" and the current one was the "one-five plan" which employees demonstrated to me with the middle finger of one hand and all five of the fingers on the other hand. The executives in the room laughed nervously. I then asked if they had an idea of how many of those 21,000 employees were excited by their "one-five plan."

I pointed out that only a few executives and managers were deciding how to reduce expenses, leaving out over 20,000 people who could probably do it better. They never considered that employees could get excited about and contribute to significant cost reduction.

In spite of the fact that the term *downsizing* has been around in business for over 30 years, for 30 years the articles on its effects have consistently showed it to be a questionable practice. The April 9, 1990 edition of *Fortune* magazine had cost cutting as its cover story (Henkoff, 1990). A major conclusion of the article was, "So far, downsizing just hasn't delivered." The story reported on a survey by the Society for Human Resource Management of 1468 restructured companies.

They concluded that employee productivity either stayed the same or deteriorated after the layoffs. The reporter said that after the layoffs employees were not working harder or smarter. I am afraid that almost 20 years later the results are no better. From a behavioral perspective, the reason that downsizing continues is that the immediate effects of the downsize decision overpower recommendations to take alternative action that only produces future, uncertain consequences.

The remedy is not unlike that presented to Ulysses in Homer's *Odyssey* as a means of avoiding the temptation of the sirens' songs which lured the sailors to steer the ships onto deadly rocks and certain death. He was advised to put wax in the sailors' ears so that they could not hear the seductive songs and to have the sailors tie him to the mast so that he couldn't take over and steer the ship himself. Knowledge of behavior provides managers with the tools to resist short-term solutions that provide an immediate, positive impact but often create significant future, negative impact.

WHAT TO DO INSTEAD

The first thing is to never let your company find itself in the situation where such action is necessary. Of course, this is easier said than done. One of our customers said recently that five years ago they had 5000 employees producing their product and today with computerization of the workplace, they are producing more products with only 500 employees. Since these kinds of changes are to be expected, action could be taken to deal with them in a way that avoids much of the downside of downsizing. I recommend the following.

1. **Involve all employees in how to solve the problem.** A number of years ago when the country was in the middle of a recession, maintenance technicians at Lincoln Electric volunteered to go on the road and sell equipment to shops that the sales force did not have the time to call. This contributed to pulling the company out of a very difficult time. (In over 100 years of existence, Lincoln has never had a layoff.)

   Ralph Archer, a department manager in a large manufacturing company, saw the economic handwriting on the wall and, although the company had never had a layoff, he knew that belt-tightening was imminent. He gathered all employees and shared his concern and the need for serious cost reduction. Not only did the employees make dramatic savings in expenses by doing such things as taking on maintenance tasks previously done by contractors, but they actually reduced head count themselves. The employees figured out a way to eliminate jobs since Ralph promised the incumbents that he would find them an equal or better job somewhere else within the company or in another company.

   In an insurance company where many of the employees were second-income earners, significant numbers of them took time off without pay while others voluntarily reduced the number of hours they worked until the business picked up again.

   There are doubtless many other stories like this where employees have contributed similarly. Head count reduction should be the last move taken by management to solve economic problems, not the first.

2. Develop a culture of lean. Thomas Gilbert, founder of the field of performance technology and author of *Human Competence* (1978), said, "Cost cutting is simply a recognition that higher degrees of incompetence are acceptable in good times when the customer is able to bear the cost." While this statement may seem a bit harsh, why is it that organizations can find a way to trim costs when faced with severe economic consequences, but not when times are good?

Why is every organization not at the right size for what they do, or at least not far from it? What incentive do employees have for eliminating waste? While the threat of the loss of a job seems to be a sufficient motivator, it seems so only to those who don't understand the effects of immediate vs. future reinforcement. The threat of another layoff probably increases the behavior of looking for another job more than it increases better performance. Threat of another layoff no doubt increases feelings of depression and hopelessness which is more likely to increase the downward performance spiral rather than stop it.

Every organization should motivate employees in such a way that they are continuously looking for ways to do things more efficiently. They will predictably do this when management makes it to their advantage to do so. The model of Ralph Archer is one that can be copied everywhere. He didn't give raises or bonuses. He knew how to motivate people and he could teach others to do the same.

Lean Manufacturing has been demonstrated to save

significant amounts of money through its processes of eliminating waste. This process focuses on eliminating non-valued activities, not non-valued employees.

In his book, *Lean Manufacturing That Works,* Bill Carreira (2005) conducts an imaginary conversation with Mr. Big. "How much can I cut my head count?" asks Mr. Big. Bill answers, "If your mission is simply head count reduction, I suggest you think about the larger issue. As you embrace a lean philosophy throughout your organization, you will reduce inventories, greatly increase your sales generated per employee, eliminate your quality issues and expense, and improve customer satisfaction levels to unprecedented highs. This will allow you to reduce your pricing, if necessary, and take a much larger percentage of market-share. As you know, anyone who currently wants to purchase the product you and your competitors make can readily do so. The question is, from whom? The only way for you to grow and obtain more sales is to take them away from your competition."

"If you are content to simply downsize your head count, the morale of your remaining workforce will be poor, your performance will ultimately suffer, and your company will become weaker. Granted, you may experience the short-term illusion of being more profitable, but this is not an acceptable endgame strategy. To become stronger and healthier as a company, you must have a strategy of growth. As you take orders away from your competition, you will grow, become stronger and healthier as a company, and ultimately increase your head count. You may double your head count while you quadruple your profitability. When I said that you would eliminate jobs, I didn't mean within your company, I meant in the workplaces of your competition. That's the game . . ."

Lean initiatives are able to consistently generate huge savings by reengineering work processes. One of the shortcomings of Lean is that it doesn't take full advantage of behavioral processes and consequently the energy and enthusiasm for the initiative is often lost after an initial wave of projects. With knowledge of behavior analysis, consequences can be built into the initiative that will maintain a high level of activity and interest until it becomes a dominant characteristic of the culture.

3. **Take care of the victims.** How well you treat those who are terminated will determine how much money and time is wasted by a downsizing. Be generous with severance pay and resources for helping former employees find good jobs elsewhere. The survivors will be looking at what you do. How they think the terminated employees have been treated will determine in large part how they will respond to helping you out of a difficult time. Money spent on severance pay, assistance in finding employment, and training for other jobs is a good investment for the future of the business.

4. **Take care of the survivors.** Do not hesitate to increase positive reinforcement from the first day of the downsized workplace. Since there is always more work with fewer people, there are many

opportunities for providing positive reinforcement and recognition for those taking on additional tasks and helping others. Reinforce suggestions, ideas, and any efforts to make things better. Set goals for improvement and celebrate successes on a daily basis. I have been told by many employees that they didn't feel right celebrating in the workplace when friends and neighbors were out of a job. However, if you don't do something to create energy and excitement about the challenge ahead, current employees will likely become the victims of further cuts.

In summary, fluctuations in employment levels are inevitable. In order to avoid wasting time and money, plan for these fluctuations by creating a culture of rightsizing to make downsizing a very rare event indeed.

o   o   o   o   o   o

#13
MERGERS, ACQUISITIONS, AND OTHER FORMS OF REORGANIZING

We trained hard—but it seems that every time we were beginning to form up into teams, we would be reorganized. I was to learn later in life that we tend to meet any situation by reorganizing, and a wonderful method it can be for creating the illusion of progress while producing confusion, inefficiency and demoralization.

–Gaius Petronius, AD 66

Mergers, acquisitions, and other forms of reorganizations have increased dramatically over the last decade, and with increased globalization they will continue into the foreseeable future. However, if they are done in the same way in the future as in the past, millions, no billions, of dollars will be wasted. Indeed, Pfeffer (2007) quoting a study on post-acquisition performance of mergers states that, ". . . as many as 70 percent of all mergers are bad for the acquiring company." It seems that the only ones sure to benefit are the deal makers.

In all mergers someone has made the case that the new organization will ultimately increase shareholder value and that the deal looks good on paper. Even when this is done, most mergers still fail to live up to their promise. In this chapter, let's accept that they all have had sound due diligence and the deal makes sense.

No one goes into a merger thinking it will be easy. Changes will have to be made in all parts of the new organization. Bumps on the road are expected and provisions are made in the plan to pay for them. Built into most merger plans is the assumption that results will not be seen quickly and indeed the plan usually states that it may take several years to reap the full advantages of the new organization. Although no merger is planned without consideration of the effect the deal will have on the employees of both organizations, the economic considerations are top priority when, in fact, in any merger people considerations should trump financial ones because people can make or break any plan. However, the reality with mergers is people considerations never trump financial ones. This reality discounts the impact that the organizations' employees can have on all M&A assumptions and leads to considerable waste of time and money.

THE POWER IS WITH THE PEOPLE

Many decision makers have apparently bought the notion advanced by Dr. Deming that the employee plays a minor role in results if the systems are designed properly. My 40 years of working with companies show me that this is far from the truth. Employees can defeat any plan or system.

In Deming's famous marble demonstration, he would ask someone to put a paddle with one hundred indentations on it into a box filled with marbles. He then asked them to use the paddle to pull out only white marbles. However, they always pulled out white and black marbles. With this demonstration, he made the point that as long as there were a significant number of black marbles in the box, the probability of pulling out only white marbles was very low. Therefore, no matter what the performer did, there would be defects (black marbles). His point was that as long as the system produced defects, the employee played a minor role in improving quality. Many acquisition or reorganization planners seem to take a similar position in that, if the financials make sense and if the systems and processes are properly designed, the people part will not be a deal maker or breaker.

Contrary to Deming's impactful demonstration that employee behavior is practically irrelevant to improving quality, the knowledgeable observer of behavior knows that the employee controls almost everything. If the employee refused to put the paddle in the box, nothing would be produced. If he put it in upside down, nothing would be produced. If he jerked it as he pulled it out or tilted it, little would be produced, and in the end it will be employee behavior that will take the defects out of the system.

This example points to the fact that no matter how much sense a deal makes on paper, it can be undone by those who are charged with producing results at the frontline of the organization. In any reorganization if the employees don't like a certain system or process, it will prove to be a huge waste of time and money. Although I don't see the people issue as a complete deal breaker, it must be taken into account when making a deal. Ideally there should be a plan to address behavior change as soon as the merger or reorganization is announced.

Every day that it takes to change opinions and behavior is a day that adds to the cost and increases the waste of time and money. In such a scenario, managers who understand behavior have a significant advantage over those who don't. While most M&A plans include meetings with employees to talk about how the deal will be better for them, they will leave the meeting to face multiple punishers created by the deal. While executives talk about positive changes, those changes are all in the future (and probably uncertain) for the employees. However, almost all of an organization's changes have an immediate negative impact on the frontline performers.

TURNING NICs INTO PICs

The punishers range from significant (job loss) to many small and seemingly trivial ones, trivial to all but those involved in them. The number of meetings increases dramatically and most of the employees feel that these meetings are a waste of time. Paperwork is multiplied. Mistakes are frequent. People become suspicious of every decision. People get angry. Feelings get hurt and it takes time to smooth them over. New people will have to be included on every communication. Some, who are left off, may get their noses out of joint. Some who are on the list don't want to be bothered. Many times a day people will want to talk about the latest rumor of who is going to be terminated or what changes will be made to the organization's structure. As these activities occur, the real work of the organization remains to be done.

Since all of these things are occurring while managers are spending long hours on integrating systems and processes, there is almost no time left to make sure that all employees are benefiting from the new organization. Managers involved almost always think that these issues can be dealt with later, but spend a lot of time reassuring employees that it is a good deal for the company and for them. However, the joke among the frontline employees is, "Is it better, yet?"

Mark Jordan, managing partner of VERCOR a mid-market investment bank based in Atlanta, is quoted in an article by Tom Barry (2008). Jordan says, "Culture clash is why most failed deals don't pan out. When companies are not properly integrated, it's often because of what's not done in advance of the sale. People will think a merger makes sense financially, and they'll pursue all the financial elements of the deal. But they won't be looking for a culture that lines up with theirs."

I agree with Jordan's points except that he seems to assume that cultures are static. If cultures line up, that is all the better. If they don't, they can be changed so that they do, and in a short time. If the deal makes sense financially and otherwise, one should be able to create a new culture that will be successful. Cultures are simply the typical patterns of behavior that characterize a group of people. When you know how to change behavior you can change a culture quickly and efficiently.

Tom Barry writes, "The clash of company cultures after the sale often dooms the relationship . . . When merged companies fail to perform, the failure almost always begins in how the organizations view their most unpredictable, most volatile and most important combined asset, their people." If he is right, and of course I think he is, then there must be something wrong with how organizations plan and implement the people side of mergers and acquisitions since so many fail.

WHAT TO DO INSTEAD

A number of years ago the president of the fibers division of a large glass manufacturing company called me for help with several planned foreign acquisitions. He related to me that they had purchased a company in Holland several years earlier and that it had been a disaster. The loss had been close to $100 million. He said that they certainly could not afford to replicate that experience and since we had been successful in changing the culture of his two plants, he wanted our help with the new acquisitions. We took on the assignment and helped them merge companies in Europe, Asia, and South America.

The first thing we did was to define the existing culture. This meant that we had to get specific about the processes, systems, procedures, and behavior they wanted the acquisitions to adopt. Then we had to define the tasks and behaviors that were necessary to make those transitions. Next we had to design consequences for the behaviors that would cause employees in both organizations to be enthusiastic about the new organization. The following is a brief description of what we had them do.

1. **Establish yourself and your company as a positive reinforcer to the acquired organization.** Pair yourself with things that are important to all employees. Spend time listening and observing and very little time talking, other than asking questions.

    a. Ask people about policies and procedures that they like and those that they think are a waste of time.

    b. Let them teach you something. Discover things that employees think they do well and things that they think are problematic and should be eliminated. Almost all organizations do some things well. Find those things and have people show and tell you what they do. A frequent question should be, "Will you show me how you do that?" Find some things that the acquired organization does that you can incorporate into the new organization. More often than not, most acquired companies will have best practices that when combined with existing practices will become even better.

c. Set up a cross-companies team for the purpose of developing a new vision and common mission for the two. Agree to procedures that will remain the same and procedures that will be completely integrated into a new way of doing things.

d. Develop a way to visualize progress on the integration so that all employees will be able to track progress. Maintaining a public, graphic display of progress introduces some external accountability on the team to make steady and rapid progress until all is done.

2. **Compile a list of burdensome rules, regulations, processes, and policies that are currently being done by the acquired organization that seem unnecessary, redundant, or too time-consuming and that can be revised quickly or eliminated.** Do the same with the acquiring company and make sure the same lens is applied to both companies. The goal is to make a stronger union, not a dismantling of the acquired company's approach. Remember, you bought the company for a reason. Keep that reason at the forefront of all changes.

3. **After steps 1 and 2 have been done, the president should communicate the vision to employees, not in bland generalities or hyperbole, but with specificity.**

Emphasize the new learning, the joint agreement of what will change, and what will remain the same. People tend to see change as a bad thing—something that is risky and uncertain. Talk about where the company is headed short and long term. But in order to demonstrate that the talk is not all talk, tell the employees of some changes that are beneficial to them that will be implemented on the first day after the transaction is complete. Eliminate some of the paperwork, approvals, and procedures that the employees feel are unnecessary and that you feel can be eliminated as well. Start positive gossip on day one. Tell stories that make it real. Be careful not to make it trivial. Plan meetings at all levels and have senior leadership show up to take questions and to convey commitment—whether in town hall, TV sessions, or face to face. Be open to additional suggestions and implement them as quickly as possible.

4. **Observe managers in meetings and with employees to assess their leadership behavior.** Observe their language, demeanor, and the reactions of their employees to what the managers do and say. Take quick action to train or remove managers who have poor people skills.

5. **Spend time understanding the positive reinforcers of the most experienced and critical leaders, formal and informal, in both organizations.** Make sure that you provide adequate positive reinforcement to them very early in the process. These are people who will likely leave if their first experiences are negative. Even more devastating, if they leave, they

often take others with them.

6. **Set very achievable targets for short-run success.** Employees in both organizations need to experience substantially more positive reinforcement the first day than they were used to in the old organizations.

7. **Discover inefficient and ineffective management practices and those who use them.** Address them immediately. Train or fire. Be selective in who you terminate. By firing the right people you gain instant credibility. Conduct anonymous surveys by an outside company so that employees can give you data that you would not otherwise get from interviews.

8. **Set short-term goals for merging procedures and policies.** Examine all policies and procedures in the light of the things discussed in this book. It is a good time to overhaul policies, processes, and procedures in line with what is known about human behavior.

9. **Employees from both organizations should be charged with minimizing waste and maximizing efficiency by examining all processes, and procedures to create new methods that everyone can support.**

10. **Make sure that ideas about how to make the new organization more efficient do not result in the loss of jobs; or, if it is done, the company should make sure that the people leaving get a better opportunity somewhere else.** Assign people to this task and reward them for finding good jobs for employees who have been terminated.

When you approach mergers, acquisitions, and other forms of reorganization with employee behavior as top priority and plan from the beginning how employees will be better off in the new organization from the moment the deal is done, large amounts of time and money can be saved. Integration of systems, processes, and procedures will offer many opportunities for positive reinforcement and celebrations around the creation of a new, better, more efficient organization. People never resist being a part of a more positively reinforcing workplace. When the challenge to employees is to make a new and better organization out of two old ones, it is difficult to resist responding in an enthusiastic manner. By doing so you will capture the hybrid vigor that comes from the effective merger of different cultures.

o   o   o   o   o   o

PERFECTLY MOTIVATED EMPLOYEES

The only happiness brave persons ever trouble themselves in asking about is happiness enough to get their work done.

–Thomas Carlyle

For many managers, perfectly motivated employees are people who do what they are paid to do. Because these managers have so much trouble getting things done, they are satisfied if employees do just what the job description states. For me, perfectly motivated employees are those who do more than they are paid to do. They are people who do what needs to be done to move the organization to fulfill its mission. They are excited about what they are doing regardless of what it is. They don't give up easily; they are constantly seeking ways to do things better, cheaper, and faster. They are willing to work long hours and never complain. If you

155

believe the results of the systems that most companies use to evaluate employees, far less than 10 percent fall into this category.

However, I suggest that *most* people fall into this category, but you have to look elsewhere for evidence of this. These same individuals who fail to exhibit the behavioral chacteristics of a perfectly motivated employee while at work are transformed once they leave the workplace. They become perfectly motivated to pursue their non-work interests. They may be collectors, sports enthusiasts, video game players, volunteers for civic and religious groups, basement inventors, or may be involved in an almost endless number of hobbies. To spend time in these activities, they make compromises on family and social relationships and even the family budget. They read, practice, and attend educational opportunities to improve their skills and knowledge. They talk excitedly about their interests and willingly and enthusiastically share their knowledge and expertise with others. They may assume leadership roles in a religious, civic, or educational group where they take responsibility for tasks, committees, and anything else that needs to be done. They do all of this without pay and, more often than not, use their own money for expenses. Many of these are the people who managers and co-workers regard as not highly motivated.

HIGH PERFORMING HOBBYISTS

Why do they act differently in their spare time? The common sense answer is that they are free to pursue their interests. In other words, they can do what they want to do. True, but when you look closely at what people do in their spare time you see that they are doing many of the same things they do at work. Every hobby, sport, and civic or religious pursuit is filled with frustrations, setbacks, re-work, and mindless repetition. Yet somehow these situations do not cause people to become depressed, cynical, and negative, as they might at work. Rather, in response to the challenges of their avocations, most people become *more* motivated. It seems obvious, therefore, that the difference between work and play is not simply that different kinds of behaviors are involved.

I am obsessed with golf in my old age and spend a lot of time with other golfers. I have heard many of them say that they would love to be a touring golf professional. Interestingly, when you look at what is involved day-to-day in professional golf, it is really just another job. Pros spend long hours every day in practice that is highly repetitive. They work weekends. They spend most of the year away from home, living in hotels and motels. Sound familiar? It gets worse. Pro golfers find their free time curtailed by sponsors who demand personal appearances and by fans who interrupt their meals and social conversations. They work under unpleasant conditions—heat, cold, and rain, punctuated by the occasional heckler. Their co-workers, the other pros, are not really interested in their success. They fail repeatedly, missing the cut and often performing poorly relative to the other golfers. They must adhere to very strict rules and regulations. Excuses are not accepted. As for the money involved, here is what Wikipedia says:

> But for the less successful, tournament golf can be an unstable profession. It is also an expensive one to participate in: tournaments have entry fees and practical costs such as travel and lodging expenses, as well as paying for a caddy. Moreover, most tournaments have a cut midway through, in which the bottom half of

players with the worst scores are eliminated. Only those players remaining after the cut earn any prize money at all. Thus, after costs are taken into account, lesser-known tournament golfers who are playing erratically (and do not have a steady income from endorsements) can be in dire financial straits in a bad year.

In spite of all this, there are thousands of people working at being a touring pro. Why would they do it when it is *just another job?* The answer: golf is a game, and games evolved very differently than most other jobs.

Games evolved by developing rules, activities, and processes that *cause people to want to engage in the behavior of playing the game.* Work evolved because people were needed to do it. In organizations, the work came first. In sport, the behavior came first.

Imagine the genesis of a game: A person starts kicking a ball. A friend asks to kick it also. After chasing the ball for a while, they decide that it would be more fun to see who can kick it between two trees in the distance. Seeing that they are having fun kicking the ball, others ask to join in. Someone suggests that rather than using trees, why not put some poles in the ground on each end of a field and because of the number of people who wanted to kick the ball, why not divide the number and form teams? To keep the game in a manageable area, someone suggests that they draw boundary lines. I need not go on. Before long, soccer (or baseball, or football, or golf) has evolved. In every game, the intent of nearly every rule and regulation is to make the behavior more fun.

The rules and regulations of work did not evolve to produce fun for the employee. For example, working on an assembly line did not evolve in the same way as playing a game. Henry Ford needed a way to mass produce his automobiles. In other words the cars were important first, and assembly lines were invented as ways to produce cars. The behaviors were an afterthought. Similarly, nobody ever just played around with cleaning products and toilets for fun. Clean toilets were deemed important first, then steps were taken to convince some people to make them clean.

Games and work have one thing in common: they both involve attempts to get people to invest a lot of effort in behaviors that they might not engage in otherwise. In every game, the purpose of most rules and regulations is to make the behavior more fun. Unfortunately, as illustrated by the 13 unprofitable management practices described in this book, those who design the rules and regulations of work often take a different approach—with dramatically different results.

The scientific explanation for why people love games is because, by design, they produce high rates of positive reinforcement. The reinforcement in games conforms to what we know makes it effective: it is personal, immediate, contingent, and frequent. I need not go into a lot of detail about the reinforcement involved in a game. Hitting a ball and seeing it go where you intended is positively reinforcing in any sport. Team members and spectators are liberal with their praise. Records of accomplishments are kept so that the event can be relived later. And so on.

Now think about the average person in the workplace. How many concrete opportunities does she have to see her accomplishments every day? Does she have a record of what she has done so that she may show it to others or review it herself? Are her accomplishments regularly celebrated by the work community? There are many good shots in every golf foursome. Every good shot is celebrated by the players. How many good shots do you see at work every day? Work is typically not organized to see them, track them, or celebrate them.

Examine the behavior of the perfectly motivated person and you will find reinforcers, or a reinforcement history, that resembles what is found in most games. Rarely is the perfectly motivated person someone who is perfectly motivated in every situation. Rather, they are perfectly motivated in some situations, less so in others. Once we realize this, the question before us shifts from, "Why are some people more motivated than others?" to "Why are some situations more motivating than others?" Companies who seek perfectly motivated employees should concern themselves with creating perfectly motivating workplaces.

A GAME CALLED WORK

If we had perfectly motivated employees, what changes would we see in the workplace? We would not need employee of the month, because you would be unable to choose one who was better than another. We would not need stretch goals, because everybody would already be doing as much as they could. What would be the point of performance appraisal? There would be no need for ranking of any kind. Almost all of the 13 management practices discussed in this book would be unnecessary. Think of the time and money that can be saved.

Can we create perfectly motivated employees at work? The fact is that most employees take a job with the intent of doing the best that they can. Unfortunately what happens is that time on the job tends to diminish motivation rather than increase it. Most organizations have systems that are designed to reward only a relatively small percentage of employees and as a result only a small percentage are highly motivated. How many companies are started when one or more employees left their employer because they didn't feel that they were fully appreciated for their contributions?

In the management literature you will read a great deal about the need for empowerment, involvement, and ownership in the workplace. All of these things are attempts to retrofit positive reinforcement into work. The fact that these initiatives are so popular is evidence of the fact that most workplaces are poorly designed from a behavioral perspective. The fact that new solutions are constantly being proposed is evidence that most of them are hit-and-miss from a reinforcement perspective. Let's start with the latter point. Believe it or not, not every employee wants to be empowered or involved. Unlike the teams in sports, many work teams are not a source of reinforcement, but rather of frustration, boredom, and punishment.

To make matters worse, initiatives that are implemented to make work more reinforcing are often superimposed upon dysfunctional systems and processes. They usually require that employees find or create reinforcers in the face of systems, processes, and management practices that in one way or another punish or ignore the very behavior the initiatives are designed to accelerate. In most cases, they are doomed to fail.

The answer to the question, "Can we create a workplace where all employees are perfectly motivated?" is "Absolutely, yes." Yet doing this requires more than the behavioral bandaids that are the focus of so much management hand-wringing. To build a perfectly motivating workplace requires that the entire system be designed around assuring that valuable behavior is reinforced at the right time, in the right way, for the right things and at the right frequency. This cannot be done without an in-depth understanding of behavior. As Bacon and Pugh (2003) state in their book, *Winning Behavior:*

> The endless cycle of innovation and imitation causes competitors to erase each other's competitive advantages virtually as fast as they can be created... One area of differentiation, however, is difficult to copy, even when competitors have benchmarked your company and learned your best practices. That area is behavior. Behavioral differentiation is difficult to copy because it requires more skill and will than many companies possess—even when they know what you are doing!

Throughout this book, I have pointed out the problems with a few of the practices that waste time and money and I have listed some of the things that can be done to change or eliminate them to make management more efficient and effective. I hope some of what you have read will encourage you to develop the skill and the will required to differentiate your organization from those organizations that are managed based on limited knowledge about behavior and therefore cling blindly to practices whose primary virtue is that they are popular in other companies. This is management by common sense, and common sense is not common and is often wrong.

Of course, common sense is sometimes right, but unless your organization is satisfied with unremarkable results, you must seek something more. Remember, science *starts* with the insights of common sense, and it provides this *something more.* In answer to the question of why people get heavily involved in golf, common sense tells us: because it is fun. The behavioral scientist takes a step further and asks, "What makes it fun?" The answers to *this question* provide tools that make it possible for nearly any workplace to become perfectly motivating.

To go beyond common sense in your role as manager requires you to become an expert in human behavior. If you put in the time and effort to differentiate yourself behaviorally, the rewards will be positive and certain for you and your organization and there will be no end to what you can accomplish. Take the advice of Thomas Carlyle when he said,

*"Go as far as you can see,
and then you will be able to see farther."*

o   o   o   o   o   o

THE 13
MANAGEMENT PRACTICES
THAT WASTE TIME AND MONEY

APPENDIX

PERFORMANCE MATRIX

This is an example of a completed performance matrix. A score of 5 is the baseline performance. A score of 10 indicates goal performance. Scores from 11 to 13 are overachievement. Scores on the various performances can be anchored by counts, checklists, or BARS.

Anchors and their values can be changed as often as conditions change, but I recommend that you not change more often than monthly. If a new process is introduced on the job, you can very easily change the scores and their corresponding anchors to reflect this.

As priorities change, the weighting of the various items on the matrix can also be changed. The weighting represents the percent of time that a person should spend on any particular performance or behavior. Although weighting is rather difficult to do in the beginning, it is of considerable value to the performer and the boss. Practice and adjustments during early attempts will improve your skills in determining weighting.

From the organization's perspective, the ability to shift weighting allows the company to rapidly shift the focus of performance to meet the changing needs of internal and external customers as well as changes in the work unit itself. An item that may have had a 10-point value one month may have a 30-point value the next month because of a customer emergency. Because of a shift to a new process, production may be minimized while yield may be emphasized. These shifts can be easily accommodated on the matrix by changing the weighting of those items.

With this type of system you have a foundation for appraisal and compensation systems. This matrix system allows you to accurately tie future pay and other recognition and rewards to day-to-day performance.

PERFORMANCE MATRIX

Name: A. Daniels Position: _____ Manager: _____ Date 11/1/99

BEHAVIORS/RESULTS — PINPOINTS	4	5	6	7	8	9	10	11	12	13	X WEIGHT	POINTS
Employee Contacts (Non-office)	<2	2	4	6	8	10	12	15	20	(25+)	15	195
Improve PM Seminar (Documented Changes)	<2	2	4		(6)		10	To Tracy 11/11	By 11/7	By 11/4	10	80
Complete EOM Article		Review Billie's Input		Add research		Revised draft	Final draft	Before Thanksgiving	By 11/14		15	165
Review Direct Reports' Matrices	<2		2	3	4	5	6	90% in person	75%	100%	20	220
Commitments Met (Percent on time)	<75%	Record		90%	(95%)		100%	Early			15	120
Customer Contact (from Checklist)	<3				4	6	8	12	(16)	20	15	180
Administrative (See Checklist)	<6	6	7	8	9	10	(11)	+3	+6	+10	10	100

SCORE 1060   Next Review Date 12/1/99

REINFORCEMENT PLAN

Points	R+	Comments	Plans
1000	Golf	No score below 8	Friday afternoon off
1200	Golf	No score below 10	Friday A.M. golf

Reprinted with permission from *Bringing Out the Best in People,* by Aubrey C. Daniels, 2000. New York: McGraw-Hill.

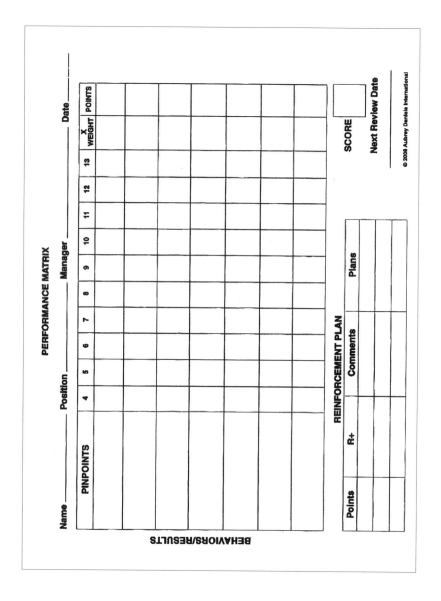

PERFORMANCE MATRIX

Name _____ Position _____ Manager _____ Date _____

PINPOINTS | 4 | 5 | 6 | 7 | 8 | 9 | 10 | 11 | 12 | 13 | X WEIGHT | POINTS

BEHAVIORS/RESULTS

REINFORCEMENT PLAN

Points	R+	Comments	Plans

SCORE

Next Review Date _____

© 2006 Aubrey Daniels International

SUGGESTED READINGS

ARTICLES

Eisenberger, R. Learned Industriousness. *Psychological Review* 99 (1992): 248-267.

Ericsson, A. The Role of Deliberate Practice in the Acquisition of Expert Performance. *Psychological Review.* 3 (1993): 364.

Skinner, B. F. What is the experimental analysis of behavior? *Journal of the Experimental Analysis of Behavior* 9 (1996): 213-218.

McDowell, J. J. Matching Theory in Natural Human Environments. *The Behavior Analyst* 12 (1988):153-166.

Iwata, B. Negative Reinforcement in Applied Behavior Analysis: An emerging technology. *Journal of Applied Behavior Analysis* 20 (1987): 361-378.

Green, L., and Freed, D. E. Behavioral Economics. In W. O'Donohue (Ed.), *Learning and Behavior Therapy* (1988): 274-300. Needham Heights, MA: Allyn & Bacon.

Nevin, J. A. Reinforcement Schedules and Response Strength. In M. D. Zeiler and P. Harzem (Eds.) *Advances in Analysis of Behaviour.* (Vol. 1) (1978). *Reinforcement and the organization of behaviour* (117-158). New York: Wiley.

Catania, A. C., Matthews, B. A., and Shimoff, E. Instructed versus shaped human verbal behavior: Interactions with nonverbal responding. *Journal of the Experimental Analysis of Behavior* 38 (1982): 233-248.

JOURNALS & MAGAZINES

The Behavior Analyst. Association of Behavior Analysis International, 550 W. Centre Ave., Portage, MI 49024-5364 | Phone: (269) 492-9310 | Fax: (269) 492-9316 | E-mail: mail@abainternational.org

Journal of Applied Behavior Analysis [JABA]. Department of Applied Behavioral Science, University of Kansas, Lawrence, KS 66045-2133

Journal of Organizational Behavior Management [JOBM]. Philadelphia: Haworth Press, haworthpress@taylorandfrancis.com

Performance Management Magazine. Atlanta, GA: Performance Management Publications, 678.904.6140, www.aubreydaniels.com.

BOOKS

Abernathy, William B., *The Sin of Wages.* Memphis, TN: PerfSys Press, 1996.

Abernathy, William B., *Managing Without Supervision.* Memphis, TN: PerfSys Press, 2000.

Agnew, Judy, and Snyder, Gail, *Removing Obstacles to Safety.* Atlanta: Performance Management Publications, 2000.

Bailey, Jon, and Burch, Mary. *How to Think Like a Behavior Analyst: Understanding the Science that Can Change Your Life.* New York: Taylor and Francis, 2006.

Cameron, Judy, and Pierce, W. David. *Rewards and Intrinsic Motivation: Resolving The Controversy.* Westport, CT: Greenwood Publishing Group, Inc., 2002.

Cooper, J. O., Heron, Timothy E., and Heward, William L. *Applied Behavior Analysis.* Columbus, OH: Merrill Publishing Company, 1987.

Daniels, Aubrey C. *Bringing Out The Best In People.* New York: McGraw-Hill, 2000.

Daniels, Aubrey C., and Daniels, James E. *Measure of a Leader.* Atlanta: Performance Management Publications, 2005.

Daniels, Aubrey C. *Other People's Habits: How to Use Positive Reinforcement To Bring Out The Best in People Around You.* New York: McGraw-Hill, 2001.

Daniels, Aubrey C. and Daniels, James E. *Performance Management: Improving Quality Productivity through Positive Reinforcement.* Tucker, GA: Performance Management Publications, 1989.

Eisenberger, Robert. *Blue Monday: The Loss of The Work Ethic in America.* New York: Paragon House, 1989.

Ericsson, K. Anders, Charness, Neil, Hoffman, Robert R., and Feltovich, Paul J. *The Cambridge Handbook of Expertise and Expert Performance.* MA: Cambridge University Press, 2006.

Gilbert, Thomas F. *Human Competence; Engineering Worthy Performance.* San Francisco: Pfeiffer, an imprint of Wiley, 2007.

Laipple, Joe. *Precision Selling: A Guide for Coaching Sales Professionals.* Atlanta: Performance Management Publications, a division of Aubrey Daniels International, 2006.

Latham, Glenn. *Positive Parenting.* UT: P&T Ink, 1990.

Lattal, Alice Darnell, and Clark, Ralph W. *Ethics at Work.* Atlanta: Performance Management Publications, a division of Aubrey Daniels International, 2005.

Maloney, Michael. *Teach Your Children Well.* MA: QLC Educational Services, Cambridge Center of Behavioral Studies, 1998.

O'Brien, Richard M., and Eds. Dickinson, Alyce, and Rosow, Michael. *Industrial Behavior Modification: A Learning Based Approach to Industrial-Organizational Problems.* New York: Pergamon Press, 1982.

Pierce, W. David, and Epling, W. Frank. *Behavior Analysis and Learning.* NJ: Pearson Education, 1998.

Sidman, Murray. *Tactics of Scientific Research.* Boston: Authors Cooperative, 1960.

Sidman, Murray. *Coercion and Its Fallout.* Boston: Authors Cooperative, 1989.

Skinner, B. F. *About Behaviorism.* New York: Knopf, 1974.

Skinner, B. F. *Science and Human Behavior.* New York: The Free Press: MacMillan, 1974.

Skinner, B. F. *Technology of Teaching.* New York: Appleton-Century-Crofts, 1968.

REFERENCES

Abernathy, W. B. (1996). *Sin of Wages.* Memphis: PerfSys Press.

Abernathy, W. B. (2000). *Managing Without Supervising: Creating an Organization-wide Performance System.* Memphis: PerfSys Press.

Abrashoff, D. M. (2002). *It's Your Ship: Management Techniques from the Best Damn Ship in the Navy.* New York: Warner Books.

Allen, J., with Snyder, G. (1990). *I Saw What You Did & I Know Who You Are.* Atlanta: Performance Management Publications.

Bacon, T. R., and Pugh, D. G. (2003). *Winning Behavior: What the Smartest, Most Successful Companies Do Differently.* New York: AMACOM.

Bandura, A. (1994). Self-efficacy. In V. S. Ramachaudran (Ed.), *Encyclopedia of Human Behavior* (4): 71-81. New York: Academic Press. (Reprinted in H. Friedman (Ed.), *Encyclopedia of Mental Health.* San Diego: Academic Press, 1998.

Barry, T. (2008). The Clash. *Atlanta Business Chronicle.* 7–13 March: 1B.

Bateman, M., and Ludwig, T. (2003). Managing distribution quality through an adapted incentive program with tiered goals and feedback. *Journal of Behavior Management* 23 (1): 33-55.

Bennis, W. (2003). *On Becoming A Leader: The Leadership Classic.* New York: Basic Books.

Boortz, N., and Linder, J. (2006). *The Fair Tax Book: Saying Goodbye to the Income Tax and the IRS.* New York: Harper Paperbacks.

Bossidy, L. (2002). *Execution: The Discipline of Getting Things Done.* New York: Crown Business.

Brewer, A. (1989). Feedback in Training: Optimizing the effects of feedback timing. Unpublished master's thesis, the University of the Pacific. Stockton, CA.

Bucklin, B., and Dickinson, A. (2001). Individual monetary incentives: A review of different types of arrangements between performance and pay. *Journal of Organizational Behavior Management* 21:3.

Carreira, B. (2005). *Lean Manufacturing That Works: Powerful Tools for Dramatically Reducing Waste and Maximizing Profits.* New York: AMACOM.

Chow, C. W., Lindquist, T., and Wu, A. (2001). National culture and the implementation of high-stretch performance standards: An exploratory study. *Behavioral Research in Accounting* 13: 85-109.

Coens, T., and Jenkins, M. (2000). *Abolishing Performance Appraisals* (231). San Francisco: Berrett-Koehler.

Cook, E. (1966). *Percentage Baseball.* Cambridge: MIT Press.

Daniels, A. (2000). *Bringing Out the Best In People.* New York: McGraw-Hill.

Daniels, A., and Daniels, J. (2002). *Performance Management: Changing Behavior That Drives Organizational Effectiveness.* Atlanta: Performance Management Publications.

Dickinson, A. M., and Gillette, K. L. (1993). A comparison of the effects of two individual monetary incentive systems on productivity: Piece rate pay versus base pay plus incentives. *Journal of Organizational Behavior Management* 14 (1): 3-82.

Drucker, P. (1999). *Management—Tasks, Responsibilities, Practices.* Amsterdam: Elsevier Limited.

Eisenberger, R. (1985). Learned industriousness. *Psychological Review* 99 (2): 248-267.

Epstein, R. (1990). Generativity Theory & Creativity. In *Theories of Creativity* by Runco, M. A., and Albert, R. S. 116-140. CA: SAGE Focus Editions.

Ericsson, K. A., Kampe, R., and Clemens, T. (1993). The role of deliberate practice and the acquisition of expert performance. *Psychological Review* 100 (1): 363-406.

Fisher, J., Peffer, S., and Sprinkle, G. (2003). Budget-based contracts, budget levels, and group performance. *Journal of Management Accounting Research* 15:51-74.

Gallup, Inc. (1999). I have a best friend at work: the twelve key dimensions that describe great workgroups (part 11). *The Gallup Management Journal* 26 May: Q12 Item 10.

Gandolfi, F. (2005). *Corporate Downsizing Demystified: A Scholarly Analysis of A Business Phenomenon.* Hyderabad, India: ICFAI University Press.

Gilbert, T. F. (1978). *Human Competence: Engineering Worthy Performance.* New York: McGraw Hill.

Glickman, S. W., MD, MBA. (2007). Fang-Shu Ou, MS; Elizabeth R. DeLong, PhD; Matthew T. Roe, MD, MHS; Barbara L. Lytle, MS; Jyotsna Mulgund, MS; John S. Rumsfeld, MD, PhD; W. Brian Gibler, MD; E. Magnus Ohman, MD; Kevin A. Schulman, MD; Eric D. Peterson, MD, MPH. Pay for performance, quality of care, and outcomes in acute myocardial infarction. *Journal of the American Medical Association* (297): 2373-2380.

Henkoff, R. (1990). Cutting costs: How to do it right so you won't have to do it again. *Fortune Magazine.*

Hogan, R., Curphy, J., and Hogan, J. (1994). What we know about leadership: Effectiveness and personality. *American Psychologist* 49 (6): 493-504.

Hollenbeck, J. R., and Klein, H. J. (1987). Goal commitment and the goal-setting process: Problems, prospects, and proposals for future research. *Journal of Applied Psychology* 72: 212-220.

Homer, (800 B.C.E). *The Odyssey.* Translated by Samuel Butler.

Hope, J., and Fraser, R. (2003). *Beyond Budgeting: How Managers Can Break Free From the Budgeting Trap.* Boston: Harvard Business Press.

Huber, G. P., and Glick, W. H. (1995). *Organizational Change and Redesign: Ideas and Insights for Improving Performance.* USA: Oxford University Press.

Kerr, S., and Landauer, S. (2004.) Using stretch goals to promote organizational effectiveness and personal growth: General Electric and Goldman Sachs. *The Academy of Management Executive* 18 (4): 134-138.

LaMere, J. M., Dickinson, A. M., Henry, M., Henry, G., and Poling, A. (1996). Effects of a multi-component monetary incentive program on the performance of truck drivers: A longitudinal study. *Behavior Modification* 20: 385.

Latham, G. (2004). The motivational benefits of goal setting. *Academy of Management Executive* 18 (4): 126-129.

Lazear, E. P. (2000). Performance Pay and Productivity. *The American Economic Review* 90 (5): 1346-1361.

Lee, T. W., Locke, E. A. and Pharr, S. H. (1997). Explaining the assigned goal – incentive interaction: The role of self-efficacy and personal goals. *Journal of Management* 23 (4): 541-560.

Lewis, M. (2003). *Moneyball: the Art of Winning an Unfair Game.* New York: W. W. Norton & Company.

Locke, E. A. (2004). Linking goals to monetary incentives. *Academy of Management Executive* 18 (4): 126-129.

Madsen, C. H., Jr. and Madsen, C. R. (1974). *Teaching and Discipline: Behavior Principles Toward a Positive Approach.* Boston: Allyn & Bacon.

McLean, B. and Elkind, P. (2003). *The Smartest Guys in the Room.* New York: Portfolio Press.

McClosky, M. (1983). Intuitive Physics. *Scientific American* 4: 122-130.

Onion (2000). Employee of the Month Sad It's Already The 19th. 19 July 2000: 36-24. www.theonion.com/content/node/28419.

Palmer, D. C. (2006). On Chomsky's appraisal of Skinner's verbal behavior: A half century of misunderstanding. *The Behavior Analyst* 29 (2): 253-267.

Pfeffer, J. (2007). *What Were They Thinking? Unconventional Wisdom About Management.* Boston: Harvard Business School Press.

Risley, T. R., and Hart, B. (1995). *Meaningful Differences in the Everyday Experience of Young American Children.* Baltimore: Brookes Publishing Co., Inc.

Roberts, P. (1997). Should corrective feedback come before or after responding to establish a "new" behavior?" Denton: University of North Texas (unpublished master's thesis).

Schulz, A., Webb, A., and Jeffery, S. (2006). The Performance Effects of Two Approaches to Setting Stretch Goals. Atlanta: Paper presented at the 2006 Academy of Management Annual Conference.

Science Daily (2008). Doctor 'pay-for-performance' improves patient care, study shows. *Science Daily* 11 Jan.

Shellhardt, T. D. (1994). It's time to evaluate your work, and all involved are groaning. *Wall Street Journal 19* Nov. A1.

Snyder, G. (1992). Morningside Academy: A learning guarantee. *Performance Management Magazine* 10: 3.

Stajkovic, A., and Luthans, F. (1997). A meta-analysis of the effects of organizational behavior modification on task performance, 1975-95. *Academy of Management Journal* 40: 1122-49.

Stanovich, K. E. (2007). *How To Think Straight About Psychology* (8th ed.). New Jersey: Allyn & Bacon.

Stuart, R. B. (1970). Assessment and change of the communicational patterns of juvenile delinquents and their parents. *Advances in Behavior Therapy,* Vol. 8, R.D. Rubin et al. (Ed.). New York: Academic Press.

Thompson, D. W. (1978). *Managing People: Influencing Behavior.* St. Louis: The C. V. Mosby Company.

Thompson, K. R., Hochwarter, W. A. and Mathys, N. J. (1993). Stretch targets: What makes them effective? *Academy of Management Executive* 11 (3): 48-60.

Towers-Perrin Global Workforce Study (2007-2008). *Closing the Engagement Gap: A Road Map for Driving Superior Business Performance.*

Vahtera, J., Kivimaki, M., Pentti, J., Linna, A., Virtanen, P., and Ferrie, J. (2004). Organisational downsizing, sickness, absence, and mortality: 10-town prospective cohort study. *British Medical Journal* 10:23 Feb.

Wooden, J. and Jamison, S. (2005). *Wooden on Leadership.* New York: McGraw-Hill.

INDEX

ABOUT THE AUTHOR

Aubrey C. Daniels, Ph.D., is the world's foremost authority on applying the scientifically-proven laws of human behavior to the workplace.

He founded Aubrey Daniels International (ADI) in 1978 and is the author of four best-selling books widely recognized as management classics: *Bringing out the Best in People, Performance Management, Other People's Habits,* and *Measure of a Leader* (with James E. Daniels). His books have been translated into Japanese, Chinese, Korean, Spanish, and French and have been licensed in China, India, Indonesia, Japan, Korea, Romania, and Saudi Arabia.

A passionate thought leader and an internationally recognized expert on management, leadership, and workplace issues, Daniels has been featured in *USA Today, The Wall Street Journal, The New York Times, The Washington Post, Fortune, CNN,* and *CNBC.*

Daniels is a member of the Board of Trustees of both Furman University and the Cambridge Center for Behavioral Studies. He is an Associate of Harvard University's John F. Kennedy School of Government, a member of the advisory board of the College of Health Professions at the University of Florida, and a visiting professor at Florida State.

His numerous awards include the Lifetime Achievement Award from the Organizational Behavior Management Network and the Outstanding Service Award from the International Association for Behavior Analysis, which also named him a 2005 Fellow.

Daniels received his doctorate from the University of Florida, where he also earned his masters degree and was a member of Phi Beta Kappa. He received his undergraduate degree in psychology from Furman University. Daniels has been honored by both Furman University and the College of Health Professions at the University of Florida as Alumnus of the Year.

Daniels and his wife Rebecca reside in Atlanta and have two married daughters, two grandsons and one granddaughter.

ABOUT ADI

Aubrey Daniels International (ADI) helps the world's leading businesses use the scientifically proven laws of human behavior to promote workplace practices vital to long-term success. By developing strategies that reinforce critical work behaviors, ADI enables clients across a myriad of industries achieve and sustain consistently high levels of performance, building profitable habits™ within their organizations. ADI is led by Dr. Aubrey C. Daniels, the world's foremost authority on behavioral science in the workplace. Headquartered in Atlanta, the firm was founded in 1978.

www.AubreyDaniels.com

PERFORMANCE MANAGEMENT PUBLICATIONS
ADDITIONAL RESOURCES

Bringing Out the Best in People

Aubrey C. Daniels

Performance Management
(4th edition)
Aubrey C. Daniels
James E. Daniels

Measure of a Leader

Aubrey C. Daniels
James E. Daniels

Other People's Habits

Aubrey C. Daniels

Removing Obstacles to Safety!

Judy Agnew
Gail Snyder

A Good Day's Work

Alice Darnell Lattal
Ralph W. Clark

Precision Selling

Joseph S. Laipple

You Can't Apologize to a Dawg!

Tucker Childers

Behaving Well

Edmund Fantino

The Sin of Wages!

William B. Abernathy

For more information call
1.800.223.6191
or visit our Web site
www.PManagementPubs.com

REGISTER YOUR BOOK

Register your copy of *Oops! 13 Management Practices That Waste Time and Money* and receive exclusive reader benefits. Visit the Web site below and click on the "Register Your Book" link at the top of the page. Registration is free.

www.pmanagementpubs.com

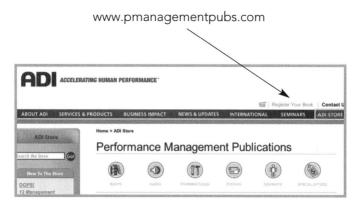

READER COMMENTS AND QUESTIONS

Interact with Aubrey on his blog at:

aubreydanielsblog.com